BOY NEXT DOOR TO FERGUSON

Do You Know Your Neighbor?

by

Edgar T. Jones

Dorrance Publishing Co.
585 Alpha Drive
Pittsburgh, PA 15238
Visit our website at *www.dorrancebookstore.com*

ISBN: 979-8-8852-7050-2
eISBN: 979-8-8852-7779-2

People don't think of each other as human all of the time. A prime example is slavery. If Black people were caught where White people didn't think that they belonged it was considered to be dangerous or even fatal just like seeing a roach in the food cupboard. When the Rwandan people began killing members of a certain tribe and calling them "CockRoaches" there was no place for the "pests" to exist among "people." I used to think that I hated bugs in my house, my bed, and especially on my body, but the reality is that I'm afraid of them and what they might do if I allow them to share the space that I have claimed as my own so I kill them without a second thought.

A live video was shared on social media when Mike Brown was murdered that I have not seen since the day it was shared. I saw the officer shoot him in the head after he was already laid out on the ground from being shot while running away. This heartless treatment could not have been committed upon an unarmed human being who was seen as a person, like a neighbor or even just a familiar face from the neighborhood. What or who did the police and the county prosecutor see Mike Brown to be when his murder was dismissed like the removal of a pest?

While the world has gotten smaller due to technology and other innovations people have somehow become less and less human to one another. We see everything through a screen that filters out feelings and essential realities like the fact that each person has a history and life connections. The challenges of life are many but that's how we know that we are alive when we overcome one at a time. Even "Forrest Gump" could see humanity in this crazy world and when Jimmy Stewart stars in "It's a Wonderful Life" the truth that every life matters has endured the test of time. I wonder what this world would be like if MLK had survived his wound and even Mike Brown. Could we have been better next door neighbors to them?

As small as this world has become no one is any further away than our own next door neighbor, so in my story I hope you see what my life was like being the "Boy Next Door to Ferguson."

Picture a small town in the suburb of St. Louis, Mo., and a nice white boy's story full of good times and family gatherings, city sponsored celebrations, and memories that were cemented in the mind of a child who grew up in Ferguson in the 60s and 70s especially when the child's parents were active in civic and political service.

The 60s and 70s proved to be turbulent times to put it politely and carried challenges for everyone who lived through them. I lived through them right next door to Ferguson and as different as my community was, I believe that I experienced many of the same things that Ferguson kids dealt with but much more and in a very different way.

My earliest memory of life was about 1957 seeing everything around me as gigantic Macy's Thanksgiving Day Parade floats. People and furniture were beyond big and I felt like no one paid any attention to me except to move me around to wherever they wanted me to go. As I grew my dreams would often take me back to the huge rooms, the size of warehouses. My body was floating uncontrollably while these godzilla sized people came and went without giving me the least bit of attention. Years

later I would awaken to a crying baby sister and bossy big brother and even bigger sister who had the last word always period.

My grandmother watched us a lot of the time and I remember having to climb the wooden stairs to her apartment on the second floor. Stairs like these were not meant for kids my size to climb because with each step I could see myself easily slipping between them and falling to my death as I slowly ascended on my way up the scary squeaky steps. The building was entirely built out of wood and it seemed old wood as I climbed like a handicapped member of an expedition to reach the top of Mt. Everest, especially in winter months when snow was present. Hayes Apartments were not very nice but when my parents both had to work it's all we had. This had to be in the 1950s because I was born in 1954 and places like that would not be considered safe in the later years.

As time passed we must have moved into a bigger house and I remember us eating in a dining room every day at breakfast being a big deal to me since bacon became my favorite breakfast food and eggs with yolk was my least favorite. My mother and I met on the battlefield of the dining room table one morning when she thought that I had to eat an egg fried with yolk in it still after I had already eaten my share of the bacon that morning. When I tried to leave the dining room she stood in the doorway. This was the only way in or out so she demanded that I eat my egg before I leave then put me back in my chair so I could eat it. My pride and freedom of choice was being challenged and my mother didn't seem to understand that the egg looked and smelled nasty. It didn't matter that everyone else was finished and already out of the dining room my plate still had an egg on it that she refused to throw away. The battle raged on as I played with the egg like it was an experimental formula used only for testing the patience of parents.

Soon the patience turned to profanity but I was determined to stand my ground. The threats of violence and various names given to the innocent egg were not going to move me from my position. After what seemed to be hours but actually were minutes the Atomic Bomb of argument gear was inserted and I heard the sound of metal and leather heading my way "Daddy's Belt" was coming so I sent up the white flag and tried to eat the disgusting white part of the egg. Choking and gagging I finally got down some of the formula but could go no further. That's when she swung the belt and missed but hit the table where I ate and caused me to put the rest of the formula into my mouth but I couldn't swallow it because it was so disgusting and even smelled bad. From then on, I asked for scrambled egg.

This would prove to be only the beginning of my challenge for power in the Jones house. Later that month I was eating breakfast with my sisters and brother while my parents had gone to the store and I wanted more bacon. My sister said that I couldn't have any more and this was an answer that I refused to accept so I made my demand more aggressively and still got a negative response.

To add insult to injury my brother and baby sister were telling me no bacon and ignoring my most serious demands. This obviously called for drastic measures and I knew exactly what to do. Since the age of four I had been watching the Lone Ranger and had learned a valuable lesson about the power of the pistol. When playing with my older brother one day I tried to use the handle of my metal six shooter to do like nearly every cowboy did to get the drop on the other cowboy. I waited around the corner of the house for my brother to peep his head out just far enough to hit him in his left temple but to my surprise it didn't knock him out, instead his head began to bleed and he cried loudly as my mother rushed him to the hospital. Later he returned and from then on he had a scar where he was hit and my gun and holster was lost. The bad guys never questioned the Lone Ranger's directions once he got the drop on them so it was clear what I had to do.

As I surrendered my attempts at peaceful requests for bacon my thoughts were on the fact that my sixth birthday was coming up soon so why not get the six shooter to do my talking for me. I saw my Daddy who was a policeman putting his six shooter in the bottom drawer of his dresser. When I went to Dad's bottom drawer, I had to move some of his clothes before I found the gun but once I got it and returned to my siblings the tone my sister was taking was very different.

She carefully looked at the gun that I had because I was pointing it directly at her while she started to huddle with my baby sister and big brother and they quickly backed into a corner of the room just outside of the kitchen. I had no sooner began to demand my bacon when we heard the sound of a car parking in the driveway. Somehow I knew that my first move had to be to put the gun back before my father could get into the front door.

Before I could even reach the dresser drawer my sisters and brother were outside telling on me and sending my mother into panic mode while I found myself a seat in front of the television set staring at a blank screen and acting as if nothing had happened.

For some reason my memory always goes blank after my dad came in the house taking off his belt, until the next day when everything seemed fine again.

That same year I started kindergarten at the Holy Angels Catholic School with Ms. Gordon as my teacher.

Here is where my older brother has been for two years now and he has done very well, so in spite of my fears I must not be afraid but I am. Somewhere in here I developed a fear of speaking in public that soon translated into an all out stammer effecting the remainder of my lifetime even to this day.

I must have been gifted in the art of pronunciation or something having to do with words because in kindergarten I was chosen and prepared to give a short speech with other class members at a nearby Catholic School's Christmas program. This proved to be a formula for disaster because all dressed up and sitting right in front of an entire roomful of people, I pissed my pants and the chair I was sitting in. Someone's mother noticed my dilemma and removed me from the room before I could give my speech but this may very well have been the beginning of my struggles with speaking.

Those days at Holy Angels were meant to shape Christ-like children but I just kept on slipping into darkness even as I was being prepared for my First Holy Communion. Having reached the second grade and seeing my older brother become an altar boy I was expected to follow in his footsteps and get baptized into the Catholic faith in this year of my education. Television had still been an influence upon my mental development and because of Sammy Davis Jr. and the "Rat Pack" I had questions about Judaism and Jesus.

For some reason I couldn't let go of a certain comments that Dean Martin made about Sammy Davis Jr. being a Black Jew and the huge laughter that followed. Sammy Davis Jr. even nodded in agreement after the statement so it seemed like something good was related to the idea of being Jewish. When the time came for my verbal request to be baptized into the Catholic faith I obviously had at least one question of my second grade teacher and communion coach. "Why can't I become a Jew?"

It felt like I had just stepped on a land mine and no one could move or it would blow up. Sister Clotilda was an older Black nun who probably was proud of the fact that we just elected the first Catholic President to the White House and Martin Luther King Jr. was a Christian leader of the Civil Rights movement so my question had to come as quite a shock to her. Nonetheless when asked to repeat the question it came out the exact same way as before and the whole communion class began to rumble with background chatter as Sister Clotilda sternly replied, "The Jews killed Jesus so why would you want to become a Jew?"

I said, " Sammy Davis Jr. is one." Sister Clotilda was highly offended by my response and quickly removed me from the class before I could influence any of the other students. Later that day the parish priest spoke with me and simply asked me if I wanted to be baptized and I told him I didn't know. From there the whole issue of me getting baptized into the Catholic church and receiving my first holy communion was put on hold and remained that way for many years later.

Now I had become a troublemaker and Sister Clotilda was watching me.

In the third grade I brought a clothes line rope to school because the cowboys on T.V. used one like it to rope cows and a number of other things. Today Mike Miller, Floyd Jackson, Milton Dawson, and Oscar Wilbert were my playmates as we began to get creative with the rope and find things to do with it other than double dutch. Mike and I went way back to kindergarten and our parents letting us go to each other's home to play. He and his family were as perfect as any T.V. family and he had several big brothers, two of whom I knew to be in the military probably like their dad. There was only one girl, his little sister Sarah, but his older brother Louis was a grade ahead of us at Holy Angels and a patrol boy. This was like the mini police force at our school and we couldn't wait to reach the sixth grade to be one of them. Floyd and I had not been hanging out as long as Mike and I but we had a good friendship none the less. He had only one older sister Wanda who was in the grade above us and a younger sister Betty. I think his father was either dead or something else and we never talked about him anyway, so I didn't try to ask any questions that might point to the differences in our families. Milton was like Floyd in that he was the younger of two brothers and their mother was widowed. His big brother was also a patrol boy with Mike's brother. His name was Charles Dawson and Charles was friends with my only brother Orville Jones Jr. even though Orville was one grade above Charles. Finally, there was Oscar who was the shortest of our group but tried to be the leader at every opportunity. His family was huge but this was because his father had children with another woman not Oscar's mom. Oscar was the oldest boy of his mom's children and his nickname was Butch, a name he tried to live up to.

Getting back to the clothes line rope and cowboys that we were playing, we had a new guy in our class whose last name was Wilkes a short quiet curly haired Mexican looking guy who was just wanting to fit in. We decided to play with him and let him be one of the bad guys since all of us were good guys. As the reenactment of last night's episode of Gunsmoke was, the bad guy was about to be hung for being a horse thief. Since we had a rope and a tree branch hung over the fence into the playground, we figured out how to make a noose, then threw the rope over the branch as we tied the hands of our convicted horse thief. I was putting the noose over Wilkes head when suddenly a loud scream was heard and we looked up to see a black shadowy looking figure floating towards us yelling," STOP! STOP!"

Before I knew it, I was knocked to the ground and the figure that had come into our midst was none other than Sister Clotilda, breathing heavily and taking the rope from around Wilkes's neck and the tree branch, then untying his hands.

At this point recess was over for myself, Floyd, and Oscar because Sister Clotilda was dragging two of us by the ear and the third following close behind to the principal's office. Here we were seated and Sister Clotilda began to describe her rescue of a helpless babe who was hanging by his neck from a tree limb as I tried to hang the babe to within an inch of his life. I was described as laughing while I tortured my victim mercilessly. Then she described Floyd and Oscar as holding the victim while he was being tied up.

While I sat there in shock speechless with my mouth wide open trying to speak but nothing coming out, Oscar raised his hand to speak when Floyd shouted, "She's Lying!" Before he could say another word, Mother Anne Marie had smacked the back of his hand with a wooden ruler. Immediately, the tone was set for the rest of the time we were in the principal's office, just as Floyd's eyes teared up my mouth slowly closed and Oscar changed his mind about speaking. We were told to sit outside of the office on the bench until called inside. Five or ten minutes later we were all three called into the office and told to stand against the wall in front of the desk.

Sister Clotilda was told that she could leave and Mother Anne Marie arose from behind her desk and walked around the front of it where she said, "Boys you could have killed your classmate. Thank God, Sister Clotilda saw you in time to stop you from doing any real harm. You need not to do this type of thing ever again so to help you obey the rules my ruler and I will help you remember that harming others is a rule that you cannot break." From her right to left we stood waiting for instructions as to how many times we needed to write something on the board but she walked over to Oscar (Butch) first.

She told him to hold out his hand as if to accept the chalk for the board but instead she grabbed his wrist and began to beat the palm of his open hand with the ruler. As a kneejerk reaction Oscar whispered loudly, "Shit!", with the first lick of his hand and as she pounded a total of about ten rapid slaps on his hand, he did a dance that resembled a person trying to resist pissing their pants at the final point of holding back the flood. When he closed his hand, she was hitting finger joints and bone rather than fleshy flat palms of the hand so I decided that when my turn came, I'd keep my hand wide open and flat.

After his punishment Oscar was sent outside of the room to finish crying or whatever. Then Floyd was next and he seemed determined not to cry but this seemed to result in more than ten licks as she tried to draw tears from him. No words were exchanged by either of them as they stared into each other's eyes like arm wrestlers waiting to see who would break first. By now I had devised a plan to either fall to the floor after the first lick or cry before ever being hit, in an attempt to seek mercy. It was easier to cry and say, "I'm sorry, Sister," than to chance getting hit somewhere other than the palm of my hand so this became my plan.

Little did I know that I was being saved for last for a reason. After everyone else was gone and only Sister Anne Marie and I were in the room she told me, "You are the leader of the pack, so you require special punishment." I tried to tell her that what she was told was not completely true but then she said, "Are you calling Sister Clotilda a liar too?" As fast as I could say it I said, "NO!" then she put down the ruler and walked to the corner of the room where she picked up a yard stick. This was not your everyday yard stick it was heavier and even more solid than the ruler was. It seemed custom made not to break under pressure. Now I was instructed to hold out <u>BOTH</u> of my hands facing up in front of me.

Now she was getting into position to begin my punishment. Just like a major league baseball player comes to the mound to take his turn at bat she stepped up to the position and measured off the proper distance needed to hit my hands with the most power. She rolled up her sleeves and threw back the part of her headpiece that was like a scarf hanging off of her head as white girls' hair did when it was too long. The only thing missing was her spitting tobacco before she stepped up to the plate.

Inside of my body I gave the order, as I had heard so many times before on T.V. i.e. Star Trek, to, "Brace for impact!" but no amount of preparation could have made these mechanical poundings painless. Each one seemed to hurt more until she started to get tired and by then the pain was constant as if they were all part of one long lasting painful blow. Needless to say, I was in tears but not crying out anything particular, like stop or I'm sorry or even I aint gonna do it no mo'. Things that I'd say when my parents gave me a good whipping. My total number of strikes with the yard stick was about 10 but after 7 I stopped counting. My palms were bright pink and throbbing as I joined my fellow criminals in the hallway. Heads hanging, we returned to our class.

Scott Street was also the street where Holy Angels Catholic Church, School, Convent, and Priest's home stood, this took up a large part of the southern side of Scott including playground and an underground Sanctuary.

This was as much home to us kids as our own houses because we spent so much time there. Every weekday Mass began promptly at 7:30 a.m. and the altar boys had to get there earlier than that to prepare for the service with the priest. I must admit that these altar boys were a special breed that deserved recognition for all that they did. Not being baptized I couldn't be one but my big brother was, so I could appreciate all that was done to perform the duties of an altar boy. In my class the altar boys consisted of Mike Miller, of course, Kenneth

Robinson, Gregory and Floyd Jackson, no relation, Raymond Bethea, Kenneth's cousin, Milton Dawson, and even Oscar (Butch) Wilbert served at one time or another. There were other boys that came and went in my class but we grew from kindergarten up together. I watched Orville get dressed in our blue pants, white shirt, and blue necktie then add the robes worn during Mass of black and white. They knew when to kneel and when to stand, how to bring the priest the wine and communion chips. They also served when the church had Midnight Mass Christmas Eve. This was a challenge especially if Mose Benny, one of the town drunks, would attend carrying his guitar that he always had but never learned to play. He and anyone else who might have been partying that night would join us for service and distract many of us from our worship, but the altar boys had to hide their laughter or hold it back altogether. There were times when Mose Benny would just join in on a hymn with his guitar and be nowhere near what was being played by the organist. At times one of the parents would convince Mose to stop playing until service was over, most of the time it would be Kenneth's dad, Mr. Robinson who was chief of the fire department.

Our service consisted of several ceremonial postures such as genuflecting as we enter or exit a pew, kneeling and standing and sitting at precise times during the Mass, and we had verbal responses to the priest as he carried out the ceremony. Midnight Mass was always a big event because it was the only night that we could stay up late and it was Christmas Eve too with presents under the tree the next morning. We very seldom attended Christmas Mass because we still had Midnight Mass to recuperate from and in my nine years that I attended I remember Fathers Schier, Forest, and Siebert pastoring the parish.

My family consisted of my dad, Orville Jones Sr. who had two jobs and was very active in service to Kinloch as a police officer at first then he moved up the ladder to detective, captain, chief, commissioner, Alderman and for a brief period after the Mayor Clarence Lee died my dad served as mayor.

Clarence Lee was very respected and educated as mayor and the night he died was an historic event.

The board of Aldermen were meeting and my dad was president of the board at that time. When my mother, who always attended the meetings came home hysterically rushing to the phone, we knew something was wrong so we began to listen closely. She described what happened in detail starting with Clarence Lee speaking at the head of the long table in the boardroom. He was in the middle of a sentence when he abruptly paused and fell face down onto the table. When my dad reached out to help him to his seat but saw that Lee had released himself of all his stool and urine. She said that she knew that he was dead at that point and screamed, "JESUS!" before making her way out of the building. Mayor Lee had been actively opposing the closing of a street giving access to Ferguson from Kinloch while in office and was considered to be quite courageous by most residents for doing that. His death automatically placed my dad into the position of mayor.

This sudden change made my dad step in for the changing of a street name. A parade and ceremony to honor the street's new name was attended by the person whose name would be given to our street, Mr. Dick Gregory, himself.

My dad was honored to give him the keys to the city at that ceremony while wearing his best attire including his .38 Special that he always wore from his days as a policeman/detective in Kinloch. This may have been the last time that I witnessed true humility in a Kinloch politician. My dad knew his limitations and never sought the job that he was doing as mayor through an election. He was content being an Alderman and having to campaign in his respective ward so when the time came to replace Clarence Lee my dad didn't even run despite encouragement from others in the community.

Mom was always right there involved in some phase of campaigning for Dad but they both held regular jobs as their primary source of income. Dad worked at Moog Automotive until he retired and Mom was the head cook for the Kinloch School District. My mom Pauline had started out working for various restaurants until she worked her way up to the position in the district. Needless to say, we finally started to eat really well as Mom got promoted to where she had access to food in large quantities. We had barbeque parties for almost every holiday since Mom ordered the food for the entire district and the suppliers would give her big discounts or gifts of appreciation for her business. Dad's work was at the factory where a lot of the negroes worked because it was rather hard and hot working with steel and furnaces that softened it for various molding processes.

Dad had one daughter by his first wife named Alice who we all loved but she was already married with her own two sons so we didn't see much of her. Next in line was the big sister of the house Brenda who had always attended Kinloch School District and was already in high school as far back as I can remember. My dad sent many a young man packing who tried to date Brenda and even pinned one of the boys to a tree while explaining the rules of the Jones house to him. Orville Jr. was my big brother. He was very smart and always a good child, the altar boy with a very creative mind for fashion and a flair for designing women's clothing. A little overweight and wearing glasses kept him from being the ladies' man he could have been but I had no problem telling his classmates where to go if I heard something bad about him coming from their lips. On more than one occasion he held me back when I was ready to fight for his honor. I fought him and certainly hurt him on occasion but I couldn't have loved him more.

Denise is the baby and was treated as just that even though she figured out early on how to milk her position for all it was worth. Skin and bones, light skinned, and a head full of hair kept her as the favorite of many people in and outside of the family. Despite her delicate appearance she was the instigator of many fights that she and I were involved in both inside the family and out.

Pauline was a true trouble maker but most of it was like John Lewis', "Good Trouble." She was always working somewhere and it would seem everywhere. I recall her being a cook at fast food joints and bringing home the best burgers ever and working in white people's homes where she'd send us outside to see the horse I named "Flicka" because it looked just like the horse on TV with its shiny red coat. We had an unspoken friendship of sorts because when I came to the fence, Flicka would come and let me touch his head or back for as long as we could be alone at the fence then he would gallop far and fast away before anyone else came nearby. I was fascinated by how rich those people must have been to have so much stuff like motorcycles, cars, beautiful homes, horses, and much more.

My mom would cook for the Kinloch School District once I got a little older and one of my favorite memories of her job that involved us kids of hers was when she had to take us to Camp River Cliff. For two weeks my mom had to cook for the staff and campers while living in a cabin just like the other campers. Here is where I got to see Kinloch junior high school kids in action but we also saw Principal Larmon Williams display the most thoughtful and organized display of leadership that I have ever seen in my life. The greatest miracle was how Mr. Williams found the money to send all of those kids to camp for two weeks for free. He had a paddle for the most serious punishments but he also showed genuine love for the students and teaching.

That love was evident at assembly, games, and particularly special events. He created songs to sing around the campfire when roasting wieners about when the student or a teacher "don't act right." The story that he told at the end of the night still strikes fear in me when I hear the tale of "Green Eyes" because he ended it with the help of another counselor who jumped out of the woods when he shouted, "Green Eyes." It sent almost the entire group at the campfire running back to the cabin area when the first people started running with Mr. Williams.

The activities were the most challenging and creative while the recreation offered fun for everyone who took part. The counselors had to be strict but even the punishment was ingenious. Boys who were caught smoking or something like that were given the humiliating task of "mopping the creek" where they had to wade in the water barefooted and fill a specified number of buckets of water then pour them back into the creek. Names like Kent Buckner and Allan Bozeman come to mind as regular creek moppers. This would only be tolerated for so long and then the camper would be sent home as a last resort. They had activities planned for rain if it happened but swimming in the Meremac River, and hiking the cliffs along the river's edge must have been among the most challenging. Everyone was looking forward to the last two days of the entire camping trip when the giant bonfire and sing-a-long happened and on the final night they had the "Sadie Hawkins" dance / party where the girls had to catch the boy of her choice to attend the dance with her. Most boys who had girlfriends tried to plan their capture but no one knew who had designs on anyone special until the running began. Some girls were uncomfortable actually chasing boys but others were anxious to catch the boy that didn't want to even talk to her under normal conditions. The party was a perfect ending for the entire trip.

I was treated like a little brother by most of the older boys and will never forget the experience. My mother who slaved over a hot kitchen from early in the morning until almost sunset rejoiced to see camp come to an end but nothing even came close to it for me in my own school days at Holy Angels.

Wilmore was the street that made up the backside of the property our parish was located on. It is also the street where the housing projects began. From our playground we could see the Kinloch Housing Authority Apartment Projects that is where many of the kids who didn't like us lived. At times while at recess we would get rocks thrown at us by the kids who didn't go to school on a day that we were in school. After school contact with public school kids was sometimes unpredictable depending upon the mood or attitudes of some of the kids we ran into. The reputation of public school kids was supposed to be as trouble makers that liked fighting but our school was the exact opposite i.e. quiet and peace loving.

Raymond Bethea, a classmate of mine, had a paper route that he handled in the Kinloch area. One afternoon I was going to the county park after doing my chores and for some reason I ran at a full gallop past our dog pen but tripped and fell after my foot kicked a 3 x 3 piece of wood on the side of the pen. Thinking that my pain was only temporary I kept going to the park with my broken toe. Trying not to limp, I joined Raymond as he delivered the remainder of his newspapers. Some of the Dunbar boys who had previously been picking on Raymond for being an altar boy and Catholic School kid saw us and crowded around as we walked. About 5 or 6 boys were circling us like a school of sharks waiting to bite and three of them had been talking about us and who we were. Pierre Williams, Pappy Tate, and Alfred Morris were the chief instigators who said things like, "You that punk ass paperboy that had a BB gun and shot at Alfred's little brother Joe, ain't you?" Raymond said, "I wasn't shooting at his brother." Pierre said, "You a damn lie. I seen you with a BB gun runnin'. So you must'a thought you was doing somethin'." Walking a little faster Raymond tried to deny doing anything to anybody but just then, Pappy said, "Y'all Cafolic School boys supposed to turn the other cheek if somebody hit you, right?"

Alfred got right in Raymond's face and asked, "Is that right, Cafolic School boy?" Raymond answered, "I don't want to fight you, man." and Alfred replied, "I know damn well you don't 'cause I'll kick yo' ass." Then he punched Raymond in the stomach hard enough to make him drop to the ground but he got up immediately and kept walking. As I walked beside them looking at what was taking place with my friend one of the boys said, "You Orville Jones the police son, ain't you?" I responded proudly, "Yeah that's my daddy." Then Alfred walking nearer to me than he was to Raymond started to say," I don't care about no police, son. I'll kick yo' ass too."

It took all of the acting ability that was in me not to limp as we walked closer and closer to my house and ultimately my daddy who I knew was at home getting ready to go to the city hall. My limp had become what was called the Cat Walk that young black men who thought they were cool would walk like. I became brave knowing that if we started to fight that my daddy would not be far away even with my broken toe. My response to the threat, as we walked down the hill closer still to home was, "Maybe, maybe not!" but to my surprise Alfred didn't start pounding me into the ground. He only said, "So you a tough mother f——-r huh?" Tough or not I just didn't see myself not hitting this guy back if he hit me, and maybe he somehow sensed the same thing so without saying anything else they all just turned around and went the opposite way. Maybe they saw my daddy or knew that we were almost at my house, whatever it was I was spared the effort of proving that I would fight.

The next day at school Raymond described the run in he had with the bullies but left out the punch in the stomach part. I left well enough alone and didn't challenge his version of the story.

There was one other time when bullies tried to push me around but this was with my big brother Orville and two other Catholic school boys that went to the movies with us downtown where all kinds of bad things could happen and most often did.

On Easter Sunday after church, we had been given money and instructions on how to catch the bus and streetcar to the St. Louis Theatre where the new movie "A Tiger Walks" was showing starring Brian Keith as the small town sheriff who had to track an escaped Bengal tiger in an area of farmers and local residents. We had on our new suits, shoes, and even dress hats, as we found our seats in the theatre. We had no idea that we'd been targeted for extortion by some local gangsters about our own age and maybe a year or two older. While minding our own business in the seats about four rows from the huge screen in the sparsely filled theatre, a young guy had approached Ernest Bryant, my big brother's classmate a few seats down from me, and demanded money but Ernest must have refused at first because my viewing of the movie was interrupted by my brother telling me to give him $2 and me asking why. Just then the scene of the movie changed from nighttime darkness to daylight. I could see a couple of dudes in the row behind us and a golf ball sized knot on Ernest's forehead that wasn't there before.

Immediately I could see fear in the eyes of my big brother as he said, "GIVE ME THE 2 DOLLARS!" By this time, I could tell that the guy who put the knot on Ernest's head was probably the same guy sliding towards me saying, "YOU BETTER GIMME THAT DAMN MONEY BEFORE I KICK YO' ASS!" On this occasion I was feeling fine and just decided that I was going to stand up and see what was going to happen if I didn't give this guy my money. In those days theatres like this had either teenaged boys or adult men working as ushers to shine a flashlight where something was out of order. When I stood up this caused the usher to shine his light on both of us and at this point the usher had recognized these boys as troublemakers from a previous time so he came towards us. The bully knew that the other boys would not say anything but when the usher arrived, I told everything I could about what was going on as the bully was escorted out of the theatre shouting, "YOU BETTER NOT COME OUT OF HERE 'CAUSE WE GON' BEAT THE HELL OUT OF Y'ALL." Looking straight at me he said, "ESPECIALLY YOU!"

While we watched the rest of the movie in peace, our minds were not considering the danger that may await outside the doors of the theatre. My brother even sat closer to me during the movie than he was before. This, to me at least, was a sign that my brother was proud of what I did in standing up to the bully. Even though he never said anything to confirm this I believe that he was.

Ernest's nickname was "Chuckie" and we sometimes called him by that name, maybe because he was the unspoken leader of the group most of the time. On this occasion as we left the building, I was leading the way to the bus stop and we ran to the bus that happened to be coming just as we came outside. There was no sign of the bullies so this was the end of any leadership role that might have been assumed on my part, Chuckie was back and talking smack. As we rode home, I had to pee really really bad and was doing a pretty good job of holding it until some jokers got on the bus talking about everyone that we passed in the bus or had just gotten off of the bus. Without warning I was laughing so hard that before I knew it, I was wetting my pants of the BRAND NEW suit that I had on. No one knew until I stood up to get off the bus and no one noticed until I moved into the bunch of us and someone got behind me to see the wet streak in my pants. By this time, we were almost at home so I just ran the rest of the way home and as I saw our driveway full of cars my mind began devising a way around the guests who would certainly figure out that I had an accident in my pants. At this point I had no choice except to wait for my brother to be a diversionary tool for me to try to slip passed the company and my parents who would surely ask how the movie was.

My mother enjoyed her company along with some Jack Black. She would cook big meals that we loved to eat and the guest loved as well. That was probably the biggest reason that she was the head cook for the school district, everybody loved her cooking. On this occasion I did something that tipped her off something was wrong when I zipped passed all of the food on the table and went straight to my room before even looking at what was there. She had some of my favorite stuff like barbeque pork steaks, macaroni & cheese, yeast rolls, potato salad, baked beans, caramel cake, and more so she surprised me in the bedroom when she caught me trying to hide my wet suit pants. This was an expensive Easter outfit because at the time silk suits were in fashion and my brother and I both had on shiny silk, mine was gold and his was blue so my mother was very upset but spared me the customary beatdown that normally would fit the occasion. I was allowed to change and still come out of my room to eat. My day went from the bottom of the dumps to the top of the world because I was hungry and could not wait to fix my plate and EAT!

Soft is not a word that anyone would use to describe my mom but kind and generous did apply. Even my sexual curiosity got the best of me due to my overconfident scheme to find out what female genitals really looked like.

About a year later at one of the card parties that my parents had I decided to hide in the bathroom tub behind the sliding shower doors and see for myself what the female sex organ looks like. When I had calculated just about when the female guest I wanted to see would need to use the facility I went into the bathroom and prepared my camouflage towels hanging on the shower doors to include a lookout position. I unlocked the door and even cracked it a little bit before laying down in the tub, the only thing I didn't think about was how to handle the odors that became part of the equation. Here came the chance I wanted but I was too afraid to look so after the good looking lady guest finished using the bathroom I was trying to get out when another lady came in right behind the first and I couldn't move or I'd be busted. Now I figured that I just need to be patient and as soon as that lady left, I could quickly lock the door and come out as if I had been using the toilet.

Seconds later I saw my chance to get up and lock the door but as I got up to lock the door, I heard my mother's voice and footsteps coming to the restroom. I dove back into the tub and tried to turn over so my lime green shirt wouldn't be noticed but that was what gave me away as my mother called my name and I automatically responded saying, "YES MA'AM." She quickly finished peeing and opened the sliding doors of the shower to find me in the tub and ask me what I was doing there. My only answer was that I was getting ready to take me a bath.

After a quiet smack in the back of my head she led me out of the bathroom and whispered to me not to come out of my room the rest of the night. I began pacing the floor of my room nervously for most of the night expecting my father to come in at any moment with his belt swinging but that didn't happen at all.

I was beginning to wonder if my mother would keep this just between us since no one else knew about what happened yet but that all changed when morning arrived and I tried to go to the only place that I knew I could find safety, Grandma's house. Having slept in my clothes including my shoes I awakened shortly after sunrise to a silent house. My mind was the only thing buzzing searching for a believable lie or a chance to escape to Grandma's house where I could call home and try to let her talk my parents out of murdering me.

My decision was to make a run for it. When I opened the bedroom door as slowly and quietly as possible it only made one little squeak but that was enough to wake my daddy who asked, "Who is that?" first and then what I was doing up that early on Sunday morning. As I was answering I could vaguely hear my mother whispering something to my dad and he quickly said, "Wait a minute, go sit yo' ass down until I get up."

This was clearly bad news and I had to make another decision as to obey the command or make a run for it to Granny's. By now my heart was racing and my fear was getting the best of me I knew if I ran that I was only going to end up at my father's mom's house and he would just as soon drag me from there as any place else. All I could do was again "Brace for impact." Soon after my decision my worst fears were realized and I heard my father say "WHAT?" then he started to put on his clothes while mumbling in his room in a loud whisper.

The secret my mother and I shared was obviously no longer just between us and I tried to climb the walls in despair for someplace to go. Everyone in the house knew that something serious must be going on and that soon the wrath of dad would come down on someone. I was the only child in the house who knew what was about to happen but my brother who had been watching me squirm figured that he would move as far to the other side of the room as possible to avoid what he could see coming.

Just then we could hear the sounds of a serious whipping in the works, 1.) The sound of dad's heavy footsteps coming our way. 2.) The jingling of his belt buckle as he took it off. 3.) The name daddy called me when he was so mad that he didn't have time to call me Edgar… "EKKA!"

This sent my brother clear into the closet where I tried to join him but he wouldn't let me in as Daddy entered the room raising his belt and aiming for certain body parts that I was trying to cover. At the same time that I was walking on the beds and screaming, "Daddy, I ain't gonna do it no more," and Daddy responding," I know damn well you ain't," and "You better not even think about doing nothin' like that no more."

This went on for what seemed like a long time to me but probably only a few minutes until my mother came in and said, "Alright Orville, that's enough, don't kill the boy." Even though my father was saying several things during the whipping, as he pulled away and gave that last stroke of the belt, I remember him saying, "You must be out of your damned mind!"

Needless to say, I was more embarrassed than anything for quite some time afterwards. My fantasies were kept in my head after that except when I got the chance to write for a class at school. Writing became a way of speaking my mind without stammering but it in no way replaced the embarrassing moments when I had to read or speak in class.

I don't know how messed up some of the other families in Kinloch were but we all did a pretty good job of hiding our flaws. The church was no different in that aspect because our nuns and the priests had families, too, but very few would comment on their lives before joining the Catholic Church. All of our teachers were not nuns or even women. Two men taught us who I remember, one was white and the most memorable male teacher I had was in the fifth grade named Mr. Kasikonis. He came right out of *The Legend of Sleepy Hollow* Ichabod Crane character. Tall, thin, wore thick glasses, had long hair, and used to comb it out of his eyes with his fingers. When at the blackboard, a voice that was a little goofy but you couldn't help liking the guy because he was just so damned nice and friendly towards everyone. Kids gave him a hard time because of his timid personality so he had to present new things to get our attention. He was the first person to introduce me to the game of chess and the various moves that each piece could make. This became fascinating especially when he described the way the game was modeled after entire wars that were fought in days of knighthood and the dark ages. He even reminded me of the one Black man who taught myself Oscar Wilbert and Alvinita

Wilson a special speech therapy class way back in third grade. Mr. Kasikonis was just so much better at displaying his passion for teaching that I found learning to be irresistible in subjects like geography, history, and English, all subjects that he taught. He embodied the spirit of the sixties when change was in the air and love was the driving force in spite of the evil that kept fighting for attention. White people who cared about Blacks were rare, but on the rise due to the many events that screamed unfair racism to us and the world, including movies, books, and news reporting that our teachers would share whenever something big happened and that seemed to be quite often. Television had become the canvas and catalyst for viewing America's need for positive change.

As we grew older, we got those positions as patrol boys and became part of groups like CYC (Catholic Youth Club). Events closer to home soon made me a more serious thinker. Death reared its ugly head in various ways and times. My grandmother died a painful and slow death, one that took the amputation of both her legs and even worse she seemed to forget that I was her best friend when she started living in the nursing home where I last saw her alive.

First Blood

On the corner of Carson Road and Scott Street after school our entire school was thrown into shock when an accident took the life of a little girl who was only in the first grade.

Her older brother's name is Lewis McDonald and the story was that his little sister was running to catch up with him as she fell in the driveway of the post office just when a mail truck was backing out at the sidewalk. The most terrible part of the incident is how the truck crushed the back half of her head before stopping. Our fire department building was right next door to the post office on the same side as the driveway where this happened but the only thing that could be done was to get the priest to give the girl her Last Rites as she lay dying.

I saw the priest kneeling at her side as I walked home. With a pool of blood surrounding her head and the truck's rear tire only inches away, the priest knelt beside the little girl who was still conscious and seemed to be looking at me as I walked past. The firemen sent us on our way trying to shield us from seeing such a terrible sight but for some of us it was too late. The vision still is crystal clear today of her laying there and her eyes following me as I passed by with the back half of her head crushed and the blood running down the sidewalk.

By this time, my father was a police detective and when he got home from his factory job he worked on the case. Things were pretty quiet around the whole neighborhood that evening but I could tell that Daddy and Mom were thankful that none of us were killed or injured because there was a still peaceful mood that dominated everything and everybody in the house that I just can't explain in words. This was one of those rare evenings when Daddy, Mom, and all of us sat in the living room and watched a TV show together after dinner and no one said a word. When President Kennedy and Martin Luther King Jr. were killed were the only other times I can remember doing that and how sad the whole family felt.

Next day at school the girls were still crying and seeing them made some of the boys cry as well. It was times like this that brought us close as a class but also prepared us for what lay ahead. What made this incident even more tragic was the fact that we patrol boys felt like we failed to do our job in helping the younger children get home safely. After that we took our jobs more seriously than ever. For a little while after the girl's death, the police and fire department would try to keep an eye on the kids after school but that ended by the next school year. The post office changed rules about trucks being allowed to back out of the driveway.

They employed Mike Miller's dad, he was our mailman for years and this made him like family because he was the one who brought us good news or bad by way of our mail. He was loved by everyone simply because he was always in good spirits and even though I could only call him Mr. Miller I knew that his first name was John. As perfect as the Miller family was, God still allowed tragedy to strike by way of Mike's brother being killed while in the military. Death was always popping up when we least expected it by way of grandmas and grandpas. All of these incidents were first and only for all of us but we got through them together as a class with our families in Kinloch.

These were the days of Muhammed Ali, Black Power, Poor People's March, The Black Panther Movement, and in Kinloch there was a group of young Black men and women who called themselves "The Black Liberators." They had a headquarters in the Bottom at a storefront where some of the most gangsterous characters would hang out. Over the years I found these same characters to be much different than I had assumed them to be. My first cousin Pete Doss was one of them and I believe that fact may have kept me from seeing a more shady side of people like William Parson, Cricket Jones, Coke Woods, and others who had a reputation for criminal activity. The Black Liberators didn't stand out until the assassination of Dr. Martin Luther King Jr. race riots, looting, and racial paybacks began to take place in Kinloch, Ferguson, and Berkeley our next door neighbors, which were mostly White at this time. That's when the headquarters got raided by county police looking for something that might threaten the safety of Whites. When some of the key leaders got arrested the group slowly faded away without much evidence of its impact left behind. The only evidence of their even being a group of people who rose up out of that era was the Kinloch Athletic Club or the K.A.C.s whom I believe still exist in some form or another. Mr. Shelton opened up an African Head Shop in the same storefront, where all kinds of Afrocentric products were sold for Afro hairstyles and stuff like incense, artwork, and sculptures were sold. The most unique afro picks around the St. Louis area were found at this store and people came from the city to buy them.

Suddenly there was something else to consider for my own hair besides the James Bond or Joe Mannix hairstyles that I had been wearing. At first some of the styles were pretty experimental and people even tried to produce Afro styles with pressing combs that just didn't cut it. Barbers began to offer Afro-Cuts and some were good and others not-so-hot. Even the women began to shock people with their short afro styles. And then came "Shaft" the coolest brother with an Afro to hit the Big Screen. This was the same brother whose face was on the jar of Afrosheen hairspray and other products.

Now I had a realistic model to pattern myself after. My dad wasn't exciting enough and was not appreciated for the many challenges he faced and overcame on a daily basis. Things like family, two jobs, discrimination, and more were not getting my attention. My mother's challenges didn't seem very interesting either since she was always there to provide meals, home remedies for sickness, working her job, and dealing with her own siblings' problems.

The next two years proved to be full of discovery. Among the neighbors on our street, we were blessed to have the addition of two kids from California living only two doors away who came to Holy Angels in the middle of the school year.

Alden and Adrienne were straight outta Compton, a section of L.A. people would soon come to know the whole world over. They quickly became the most interesting kids in town because Alden looked and acted like the most intelligent and mannerable boy a parent could have. He and I became great friends immediately because he was so far from what he seemed that I couldn't resist his mind for mischief. Adrienne on the other hand was the picture of California dreamin' every time I saw her, she had a personality to match her Hollywood swinger reputation and my dream girl fantasy.

The last days of school and summer with those two as neighbors proved to be very eye opening as far as sex was concerned. My older brother fell in love with Adrienne right away but I was busy learning all that I could about sex from Alden who was showing me how smooth he was by sweeping Rhonda Lieu off of her feet and even planning to get into her panties before he was done. Rhonda was my "Shero" so this I had to see but all I know is that they kissed. Now he was my hero as we transitioned into the summer of constant fun and mischief up and down the street. He had all of the adults thinking that time spent with him would increase my vocabulary and scientific knowledge but the mission would always wind up being of a sexual nature.

We all attended a dance at Holy Angels one fall evening and kids from the public schools and our own classmates were all in attendance. Adrienne had been going to Kinloch High in the 9th grade while Alden and I were still 8th graders but school had just begun and it was only the beginning of October when kids were just learning the ropes of the new class that they were in. The dance was going pretty well for everyone until a fight broke out and the whole thing was ended early.

As the crowds left and went their separate ways on foot, our crowd of friends and family headed south toward the "Bottom" and the other kids went north if home was in that direction. While we walked, I had to keep close to my little sister Denise but my eyes were on Adrienne as we filled the sidewalk and headed home. I was dressed to the "T" in a very stylish Nehru sport coat and white turtle-neck shirt and a neck chain with a peace symbol hanging outside of the sport coat. Suddenly one of the Kinloch High boys named Ronnie Owens or Arms (one of them) who must have been trying to get Adrienne's attention jumped in front of her on the sidewalk and slapped her in the face before anyone even knew he was there. Without a moment's thought, I forgot all about how clean I was and tried to run to her rescue but my little sister grabbed my hand and refused to let go until the guy who slapped her was grabbed by his brother, Donnie. When my sister grabbed me, I was being torn by a need to fight for the honor of the girl I loved or protecting my little sister from any violent outbreak that may occur. The next moment would determine whether my assistance was unavoidable or not.

The quiet response that Adrienne gave of standing still

without hitting back or crying is the only thing that saved the walk home from becoming the site of a second serious fight between myself and Adrienne's attacker. We never discussed the incident but it would become one of my most memorable times that I'd like to have done more for the honor of a very special friend.

Eventually, by the late fall of that year, I found myself French kissing Adrienne on the side of their aunt's house as part of a kissing game and wanting much more. Although we truly cared for each other, my immaturity and the separate schools got in the way. She was being swept off of her feet by older more experienced guys before I even knew how to talk to her, so as quickly as my new friendship and love interest had begun, they mysteriously moved back to L.A. to live with their father.

The ninth grade proved to be a year of growth. All of my Holy Angels family of friends whom I knew since kindergarten were developing new friendships at the Catholic high school named St. Thomas Aquinas where most of us went.

I kept close to my Kinloch homeys for the most part and due to my ongoing speech problem I didn't talk a lot. The few Black students that attended Aquinas were trying too hard to fit in and I almost instantly found that to be a formula for disaster. When a very plain looking white girl named Donna kept flirting with me, I thought about checking her out until on the last day of school she summoned her white boyfriend from another school to put me in my place as she introduced us out of the blue.

The one and only school bus from Kinloch was only half full of students but when they saw me standing on the sidewalk with Donna clinging to her boyfriend like she needed protection, the boys *and* girls got off of the bus ready to support me if something were to go racial and a fight start. Before this day I didn't know how much we cared about each other. As my crew stood watching and Donna's boyfriend's gang stood by smoking cigarettes, I made sure that nothing was even said to suggest a fight over what I considered a trampy white girl seeking attention. It wasn't until much later in my life that the bravery of our class against a potential army of white kids ever registered with me. My time at Aquinas was miserable and I asked my parents to let me go to Kinloch High for my sophomore year, saving them money and helping me connect with Kinloch's heritage and people who I thought were missing in my life. I knew fitting in wouldn't be easy but nothing else was easy so why should high school be.

The new friends who I made were familiar with my mother who cooked lunch every day and some knew my dad the cop. My classmates became the best friends to have especially Billy Hughes who took me under his wing and adopted me into his family. His friends became my friends and his enemies my enemies.

We shared many interests including the girls in our class and outside it. Girls became the driving subject behind each thought and action under our control. School work was not challenging at all, so school became a social club with certain restrictions that often included skipping out in the middle of the day. I admit that there could have been more focus on educational activities if I had been committed to college or a career choice but wanting to be cool led me to try marijuana and eventually other forms of intoxication at the tender age of 15. Even before I became friends with people like Billy, Henry, Walter, Punko, or James-Lee, I started spending time with kids who weren't exactly well behaved, and stealing became part of the expected past-time when opportunity was presented.

One son of my mother's good friend, Miss Gwendolyn, was Eddie and sometimes even during school hours I would follow him on his adventures. My first risky attempt at stealing anything of value was when the soda truck parked in front of Uncle Dick's. Eddie and I tried to steal two cases of the large bottles of Vess soda but as we walked around the side of the building with soda cases in hand someone shouted, "Hey," and he dropped his sodas and so did I then we both ran like crazy. My next attempt at stealing came in the form of a pay-back for having my new pair of gloves stolen from me. Ozell Wilkerson had stolen my gloves and was bold enough to wear them openly even as I asked if anyone saw my gloves. He wore them without being outside almost daring me to call him a thief. He also would wear a pair of sunglasses while sporting the gloves inside the school as part of his Mr. Cool outfit. My chance for revenge came when we were playing basketball in the gym and my team lost but Ozell had next game so as he got up and I sat down I took his sunglasses without being seen. As soon as he was finished playing, I watched him begin to look for his glasses and the expression on his face said it all.

He began to shout, "Who got my Mother——ing glasses?" and stopped the game to make sure that everybody could hear his next few sentences. First, he repeated his initial statement then promised that nobody was leaving until he got his glasses. The gym teacher asked politely if anyone had his glasses or not then dismissed the class before any new threats were made. Later that afternoon I destroyed the glasses and left them where they could be found in the hallway. My Catholic school boy reputation didn't allow Ozell to ever suspect that I had gotten revenge for the gloves that he had stolen but I felt like I had my revenge and later became casual friends with him later on.

Losing my virginity was a let down because instead of a loving relationship, sex was introduced to me at the end of a train to nowhere. One of the girls who regularly allowed several guys to have sex with her at the same time was at a friend's house when the word reached me and my crew so we ran there to join the party. The purely mechanical and quite nasty nature of that encounter and others regretfully shaped my views on women as sex objects and had been engraved in the back of my mind forever. In earlier years seeing my mom meet a man who wasn't my dad at Forest Park one summer day and being left at our cousins for hours at a time gave me cause to doubt the value of spousal loyalty. She didn't think we knew it was wrong but we did. To avoid bigger fights between my parents, we kept her secret from our dad even when she stayed out late and asked for a fight.

Then Jenny X became a target of my affection. She was popular, funny, and beautiful, but I thought that equated to a soft target for sex. To my surprise she was strong willed, mature, loving, and determined to reach her career goals. In spite of many nights of kissing and heavy physical contact, she always demanded my respect for her physical limits of the relationship. One New Year's Eve, I walked in the snow to the house where she was babysitting for our most heated physical contact of the relationship where she proved to be a woman of true inner strength and virtue. I let her get away and continued to fail in several relationships afterward.

At this point my immaturity disguised as masculinity dominated most of my decisions and cost me many opportunities for a love connection. Even into my junior year at Kinloch High, the choices I made didn't improve my outlook for a brighter future. By now I had become an accomplished thief with at least one big fight that took place during the middle of an assembly in the school gym. This happened to be a day when I was just looking around the gym and seeing a lot of kids acting like they were better than others. In the area that I was sitting in the boys close to me were considered nerds or too quiet to demand any attention except to poke fun at. Maybe I was one of them and didn't know it, but that hadn't crossed my mind because to me most of them were children of people who my parents knew and had been to our house or vice-versa. One of the most outspoken nerds who never apologized for who he was is Roger (Pee-Wee) Taylor Jr. who knew me well. His most obvious fault was being short and having some vision issues but there was also Freddie Clark who like me had a bit of a stutter but our parents spent lots of time at each other's homes. Then came the guys who had previously attended Holy Angels School with me like Michael Haulcy. He seemed to be hanging with some boys who had a bad reputation and while sitting in the row of bleachers just below me started to pick on a quiet young man whose only fault was being quiet and small and skinny.

Knowing how quiet Michael had been at Holy Angels struck me as totally unacceptable so I asked him, "Man why don't you leave him alone, Mike?" This must have seemed like his opportunity to show that he belonged with the bad boys and the next thing to happen was Michael punching me in the eye. When he hit me, my immediate reaction was to put this fool in a headlock until I could raise him up and punch him in one or both of his eyes. While I had him in the headlock, I punched him repeatedly in the very top of his head until my chance had arrived to punch him in his face but just as my fist was drawn back, we were separated by male teachers. Later on, came the after school fight that looked like all out war.

When our friend Punko was being threatened by Mark Robinson and some of his friends I chose to walk with Billy, James Lee, and others in support of Punko's right to a fair fight. When school ended that day, a crowd gathered around Punko as we walked down the hill toward home but Mark found his way to Punko and the crowd stopped around the two of them. I had picked up a stick along the way but someone commented that sticks break so standing around the two of them as they squared off to fight, I was hoping for a fair fight and it started off that way until little Joe Morris jumped on Punko's back. Like a knee jerk reflex, I broke my stick over Joe's head to get him off of Punko then all hell broke loose and it seemed like everybody was fighting somebody else. By the time police showed up and the crowd began to scatter, Phillip Jamieson had broken my elbow with a steel pipe. I tried to go to my after school job at the meat packing store but soon had to go to the hospital where a screw was surgically inserted into my elbow to repair the damage. At this point I was pretty close to my classmates and they came to the hospital to visit me and tell me about the day after the fight when James Lee brought a gun to school. Nobody got shot, but the potential for more violence was a real possibility.

Shortly after the fight one of the places where guys would hang out became the apartment of a girl who lived with her two kids but was as masculine as she was feminine when talking to guys. We became good friends and she introduced me to the girl who became the mother of my children in later years through a series of encounters that kept bringing us together after long periods of being apart. She lived with her mother and two little sisters in the projects but had strong ties to Kinloch through her grandfather and his family.

He was a preacher and one of his sons was one as well but lived just next door in Berkeley. Glenda had been mistreated by her mother's boyfriend and tried to shield her sisters from meeting the same fate but her mother refused to cut off her relationship with Mr. Jimmy, who was the symbol of evil to all three girls. He worked for a sod making company and bought his way into the good graces of the mother every time he messed up.

Glenda and I were best friends before we were lovers so I tried to be as helpful to her entire family as I could for our time together. Having a car brought some form of escape at times when I could take them for rides with me. The "Puppy Love" affair didn't last long because Glenda used to pinch me all of the time, so I stopped seeing her altogether and was clueless about what to do with my future except I went after other girls as the opportunity presented itself.

Some more serious thoughts began to cross my mind when a young man named Kenneth Campbell was killed while supposedly playing "Russian Roulette" with a couple of other guys in our class. Kenneth was a very funny friendly likeable guy whose death was totally senseless and my faith in God was far from established.

Another friend of mine, Jerry Turner, was shot but survived and now I began to evaluate my own life's value and where I was going because school was just not at all interesting enough. Skipping school wasn't even interesting so I decided to join the Army and see what that was about. Jerry Turner said that he was ready to give it a try so we joined on what was called the "buddy" plan. Later we found that to be non-existent and we were on our own.

MANCHILD

This morning was to be different from any other morning that I had ever experienced. Today I am being taken to the downtown military induction center where I will join the Army and be taken to Fort Leonard Wood, Mo., for my basic training. As exciting as this is, it is also sad because I am leaving home for the first time as a man and not a boy.

I haven't done much to prepare for the change in either location or social status. This is why I am caught a little off guard when the excitement of the day is mingled with feelings of fear, regret, and inadequacy. Before, all that I could feel was anticipation of how much I was going to change personally and come home an independent man of the world. Little did I know that in a short time everything that I thought was important would change.

After a few hours of fairly cordial treatment, reality began to set in. This was accomplished by way of the final physical inspection and the swearing in process.

In a large room that was very impressive in that there was a podium and very large American flag in the front of the room where we had to stand and meet an officer of some kind who asked that we stand at attention while he read to us the oath that we were taking to be sworn into the United States Army. We raised our right hand, and repeated after the officer word for word until he stopped and congratulated us for becoming part of the United States Government.

Immediately after the officer was finished another gentleman, or so I thought, stepped up on the podium and began to scream instructions to us about where to go and what to do. Beginning with where to take our papers that I suddenly remembered we were instructed to never put down until we were told that we were at Fort Leonard Wood next to our bunks and ready to turn in for the night. From this point on, everything we did would be done in alphabetical order using last names first. As we exited the large room, we entered a much smaller room where we sat at a desk next to a man who typed our name and social security number onto several papers that he instructed us to put inside our large vanilla envelopes. This is where things got a little weird.

We were instructed to all go into another room where we formed a circle around the entire space of the room. Here we met a man in a doctor's coat who told us to turn around and face the wall behind us drop our pants and bend over while spreading the cheeks of our buttocks. Then he said to remain in this position until we were touched on the buttock by the doctor, then we were free to pull up our pants and wait for further orders. This would be the beginning of orders becoming the word that permanently replaced the word instructions.

Upon being touched on the cheek of my buttock, I quickly raised my pants and stood facing the wall. All but maybe two of us were ordered to proceed to another room while the others were detained for some sort of questioning.

The rest of the day was full of various orders that included some that made sense and others like the buttock thing that I still don't see the purpose of. If it hadn't been for lunch, I don't think that I would have been willing to endure the constant shuffling around that became the rule of the day.

An older white guy who was reenlisting described the whole process as the "hurry up and wait" method of the military and that we might as well get used to it. Well, he hit the nail right on the head, because for over eight hours this seemed like all that we did taking smoke break after smoke break, so if you didn't smoke you were at a loss for things to do.

Finally, we were ordered to proceed to an area where we would board the greyhound bus that was on the way to pick up the new recruits, and that was us.

With papers in hand, we boarded the bus at about 6 p.m. that evening, what we thought was the end of a day that started at 6 a.m. that morning. Three hours later, we realized that we were just getting started.

The sleepy hollow of my greyhound bus seat was interrupted by our arrival at Fort Leonard Wood Reception Center where we were introduced to a rather loud mouthed Black man wearing a Smoky the Bear hat. He shouted a number of various curse words and orders all combined together as we were rushed through a process that supplied us all with a mattress, blanket, sheets, and orders pointing us where to go to find a bunk bed. Here we were given the option to freshen up in the multi seated toilet without dividers called a latrine or go to sleep prepared to be awakened at 5 a.m. the next morning.

Sleep was the only thing on my mind so that was an easy choice to make. This was November and there was snow on the ground already so the temperature was icy cold with a good chance of getting colder.

Before the sun was up, that same guy in the Smoky Bear hat came in shouting and turning on lights but this time, he wasn't alone. There were three more guys just as loud and foul-mouthed as the first guy. Chaos and total confusion ruled the next few moments while I tried to gather my thoughts and find some sense of direction. While sleeping I dreamed that I was at home in my bed and this became a nightmare until I realized what I had done. Out of fear, I sprang out of bed and gathered myself enough to go to the latrine where there was a line to pee behind each of the urinals and an odor that would choke an elephant.

Somehow, I managed to make my way to the urinal to pee then hurried out of the latrine and back to my bunk and lit a cigarette but by the time smoke filled my lungs the Smoky Bear hats were back yelling, "Fall Out" and everybody was rushing to get outside and line up. As soon as I saw that I put out the cigarette and ran out to join the others in line.

Here we were being pushed and placed by the Smoky Bears to line up a certain way before something else could happen. Once we lined up correctly one of the Smokys yelled for quiet until he got it. Then we could see why we had been lined up and called to silence.

The Smokys stood in special positions and stopped yelling. Then this older and very dark Black man wearing a Smoky Bear hat walked in front of the entire group of men and began to speak in a very loud but calm voice about who he is and what he would be doing to make soldiers out of us.

Just then one of the guys in line said something to another guy and it seemed like his movement was a magnet for the head Smoky Bear hat to run up to this guy and begin yelling right in his face. He didn't dare say a word back to this guy and we all knew it. So, for the next few minutes nobody moved or said a word. As we listened, we were told how to proceed to the mess hall for breakfast before beginning the long day's process of getting uniforms, haircuts, and further orders.

Several times during the day we all got singled out and challenged for whatever reason they could find. By the time the day was over there wasn't enough pride in the entire group to fill a shot glass. Everyone seemed to be unified by the fact that none of us was any better than the other.

This quiet atmosphere carried us into the next day or two but the pride of life soon started to rear its ugly head. Starting with the reenlistment guy, certain guys started to put down the slower guys and show others how to do things the. "Army Way." Most of what was shown to us was very useful but later it was evident that these guys were competing for leadership positions within the platoon before they were even assigned to one.

Some of the guys, myself included, were a bit put off by these guys and their self-appointed leadership roles. Soon groups of guys that had common interests and opinions just naturally formed and it was not long afterward that the unity of the earlier experiences was forgotten.

We were taught to do most of the things that had to be done in order to function as part of a basic training group of guys over the next few days. On the third day we were given assignments to become part of a Brigade, Company, Platoon, and Squad. The Brigade consisted of four Companies; the Company had four Platoons; and the Platoon had four Squads. Each squad had eight trainees.

Trainees are the point at which all of us started out, but there needed to be leaders appointed so that the various divisions could function without a drill sergeant always being present. This would soon be determined as we took our first Physical Training (PT) test. Trainees were tested on the time it took to complete a series of activities such as push-ups, sit-ups, and the mile run.

The results of this test not only gave birth to trainees with authority but now a whole new list of slow or special trainees were discovered. Some were expected but others came as a total surprise to the majority of us. For instance, we expected the slightly overweight guys to be slow but there were some who seemed perfectly fit but had no energy so they were put into this category too.

One of the people on this list was Jerry Turner, a fellow St. Louisan, who joined with me on what was called the buddy plan. This was supposed to mean that he and I would be able to stay in the same unit for our entire first year of service. As time went on neither of us had the nerve to ask why we didn't serve in the same unit. We just took things as they were.

Delta company was the unit that I was assigned to while Jerry was in Charlie company. We went to training classes at the same times and had PT in the same general area but lived in separate barracks and were in different companies. Having to sleep in bunk beds and by alphabetical order meant that my bunk mate was a white guy named Ralph Jones from somewhere in the eastern United States. He was white but didn't seem very hard to get along with so for the next eight weeks we made the best of our situation.

The next four weeks proved to be very informative because we not only learned to march salute and care for our M-16 rifles but some lasting friendships were beginning to take shape. David Hall and Jesse Hicks were two of the people from Delta company who were also from the St. Louis area. This was how most friendships were formed due to the common knowledge of places and history in a particular city or county. We even shared in some similar lifestyle activities, such as marijuana use.

As fate would have it, so did most of the other guys in the unit. This created an interesting opportunity for some fast money if we could go home and bring back some of the product that everyone was craving but had no access to. Since payday was coming soon, Jesse and I took the three hour bus ride home on the first weekend that we were allowed and brought back enough to double our investment and put a smile on every face that did business with us. If only we had been smart enough to keep our business separate from our pleasure maybe the next phase of our military training wouldn't have been so painful and life changing.

It was payday and being the cool guys that we were right after the morning headcount we chose to smoke a joint before joining the troops and marching to our first class of the day.

Our bodies had been drug-free for over a month now and our systems were overwhelmed by this potent weed that we smoked early in the morning. Myself, David, Jesse, and a few others lost track of time and even went so far as to lie down on the floor underneath the bunkbeds before falling fast asleep. We didn't dare lie down on our tightly made bunk or get caught sleeping.

We thought that as usual the company would return to the barracks before lunch and we could rejoin our unit for the rest of the day. Instead of everyone marching back in mass formation, today guys were coming back one at a time or by two's or three's. By the time my bunkmate Ralph returned and woke me up it was almost 3:30 p.m. and our names had been called to receive our pay.

All of us sprang up out of our sleep and ran down to the pay line to get paid, a process that called for the pay officer to make us sign a receipt before he counted out the cash in our hand. This was something that none of us wanted because it singled us out and brought up questions about why we were getting paid out of turn. On the way we got our stories together and thought we could get our pay and stay out of trouble at the same time. Needless to say, this was only the beginning of a long and uncomfortable ordeal that resulted in punishment and a fine of $150.

This would be an easily forgotten incident had it not been for the general direction that it pointed me toward. During the time that I was being punished, we were put on certain restrictions that kept me from going home on the weekends. The other guys were given the same punishment and we would usually sit around feeling sorry for ourselves and bad mouthing the leadership for having us pay for our mistake by taking our free time.

Being young, physically fit, and full of energy was a perfect formula for mischief of any kind that was available, especially when everyone around seems to have a negative attitude anyway. My attitude was being molded without me even questioning the logic or justification for negative feelings toward the Army. I was falling into a pit of proud self–centered boys who thought that being a man meant getting as many women and as much money as possible. Truth be told, this was already what I had been led to believe during my previous years of development in Kinloch, so my Godless lifestyle was only being reinforced by the macho-man military company I kept.

Before I chose to take advantage of what seemed a golden opportunity for personal gain, I had been a model soldier. Chosen as squad leader in my platoon, I was on the path for a leadership position and placed in a class known as the Special Leadership Preparation Program (SLPP) pronounced the Slip program. After my fall from grace, my thoughts were only on quick money, fast women, and being cool. In theatres James Bond, Shaft, Bruce Lee, and The Mack were the box office hits that helped form most people's conversations and thinking. I was not immune to these influences. Over the next few months, I taught myself to steal, cheat, gamble, lie with the best of them and I even perfected my use of Bruce Lee's Roundhouse Kung Fu Kick. To be honest my entire life was being tossed by whatever way the wind blew, air born. I thought that I was in control of everything but looking back I was being controlled by every popular viewpoint, movie character, or selfish motive that crossed my mind.

From Basic Training we graduated to Advanced Individual Training (A.I.T.) where our aptitude test scores were used to determine what job we would be trained for. I was classified as a 71B30 that simply gives a number describing a clerk-typist who should type about 30 words per minute. This change meant a change in location and friendships as well, but unfortunately it was from bad to worse. Here the guys I was being housed with were even more into drugs than the previous bunch

Home Schooled

Here was where I met Whippet O. Terrel a brother from St. Louis who was the definition of cool but in a lazy way. We had classes together and simply being from St. Louis gave us plenty to talk about. The main subject always seemed to be, "Who got the fire weed?"

These advanced training classes were not nearly as restrictive as Basic Training was, so we could leave the base at night and on weekends to find all sorts of recreation to occupy our free time.

The Mess Hall was smaller and less of a hassle to eat at because during meals we were considered on our own time. This was totally the opposite of what Basic Training was like. In Basic we were lined up standing at attention until the line moved up, and this only happened as each trainee yelled out his military status, either US, RA, or NG respectively meaning drafted, enlisted to the regular army, or a national guard weekend soldier. There was strict silence while eating inside the large school cafeteria style dining area and as we finished eating someone quickly rushed us out to make room for the next person.

One detail of the new Mess Hall was particularly noticeable and that was the music being played during mealtime. Black soldiers were especially sensitive to this detail because this was the era of Soul music that was unlike any other. Music labels such as Stax, the Memphis sound, and various other producers were just getting noticed by the Black community. The nationwide representation of Blacks on a military base meant the sharing of music from every hometown with every other home town representative, and we all liked to listen to good soul music after getting high.

We also would get a serious case of the marijuana munchies after indulging ourselves. So obviously the music being played in the mess hall was a topic of discussion, especially when the only music played was country western. Even the White boys who smoked weed objected to the absence of their Rock music which we also enjoyed including Classic songs by Rare Earth for instance.

Weekends that found us short of the funds it took to leave the base posed a problem if somehow we were able to get high but had to eat at the mess hall. One time in particular we, meaning myself, Whippet, and a brother named Darryl Virginia, hooked up with a hippie type White guy who's name isn't worth mentioning to smoke some weed. After getting stoned and getting hungry, we noticed that no one had money to buy food and the mess hall was closed for the evening.

The problem this posed was easily solved by a bit of creative thinking, in the form of finding a way into the mess hall where they always had some kind of cake just sitting around. I volunteered to be the hero for the dangerous mission and was successful in capturing a sheet cake large enough to hold us over until the next morning when breakfast would be served.

Someone mentioned that the stereo system which played the music in the mess hall was just as easily captured as the cake, so a return mission was launched but this time instead of using the same route of return I chose a door instead of the window that had been used for the entire cake mission. Someone saw me as I exited the mess hall but this was not to be a problem because the White boy had a car that he could drive us somewhere off the base to stash the stereo.

Trusting him to stash the stereo we were free of any evidence of the stolen goods and now any mention of what the witness saw would be our word against the witness's. Wouldn't life be wonderful if everything went as you planned it to go?

The long and short of this entire episode resulted in the three Black guys being put in the Fort Leonard Wood Stockade. The White guy was given a discharge for his testimony against the Negroes, but one thing happened immediately after my trial that he wasn't expecting. I volunteered to testify on behalf of the other two Blacks that myself and the White guy were the only ones involved in the burglary. This made the case against the other two shaky at best so the charges were dropped against them.

Now since somebody had to pay for the crime that was committed and my head had already been chopped off the only thing left was to do the time. This process had already begun since I was presently in the stockade. My two partners in crime were released that same day and sent me thank you notes with words of encouragement for the task ahead. My spirits were almost lifted by their words until from my barracks window I saw them being sent through the steel gate that was bordered with razor wire and guarded by armed guards in two towers. They were sent back to the point at which this whole mess began with their same rank and freedoms, just awaiting orders to go to their first regular duty station. The future that stood before me was not quite as certain especially since the rumor in the stockade was, that once an inmate was sentenced, they sometimes got lost in the system for months and got classified as holdovers awaiting transport to the destination of sentence execution.

In my case the judge sentenced me to a total of six months' time to include stockade and the period needed to complete my duties at Fort Riley, Kansas. This worked to my advantage since

I had already been in the stockade for about three weeks already. Doing time there was scary at times and educational others.

The characters I met inside were unforgettable to say the least. All of us tried to stay on our toes because we pretty much knew that everybody there either thought he was slick or didn't care about anything or anybody other than himself.

Meals inside were not very different from the mess hall. Working in food preparation was considered a privilege because of the access to extra food. Serving in the serving line was a job that got rotated among the inmates probably because of the complaints of the serving size or just the opportunity we had to talk smack to each inmate as they came through the line. I got a chance to work in the mess hall on a couple of occasions where I learned about the "BOX."

The server was given a portable container for food and liquids like coffee or juice then sent with a guard to the BOX to serve inmates living in solitary confinement. Here I was instructed to dip a serving of each item of food or liquid to each inmate through a hole that he would use to take his paper plate and cup inside his tiny living space. Until this point, I had only been warned that the BOX was not a good place to be sent. Now the reality of just how terrible the BOX is was really sinking in. The BOX was reserved for two types of inmates, the ones on suicide watch or unruly and a threat to other inmates or guards. Just having a fight with another inmate was grounds for being put in the BOX. Because many of these guys were straight out of Viet Nam, fighting could easily lead to the death of one or the other of the fighters, so it seemed a reasonable method of punishment.

In contrast to punishment, there was recreation. This came in the form of card games like spades and bid whiss inside the barracks and movies on weekends when it didn't rain. Weather was a factor because a projector was set up outside and we marched to a spot in the grass where we would sit and watch the entire movie. Every time we watched a movie it was a western shoot 'em up.

I recall every movie that I saw there and all were very violent in content. Perhaps this was just due to the times we were living in because all the movies were recent box office releases. There was one movie in particular that has become a classic since that time which may have helped to shape my future attitude about not only the army but my life in general. This movie starred William Holden who was featured in at least two of the movies I saw while there. The name of the classic was "The Wild Bunch" and the violent content was just part of the overall distorted view of life portrayed by the characters. In the end even the lives of the Wild Bunch were trashed in a hail of gunfire just to avenge the death of a fellow criminal. The other movies included such titles as "100 Rifles" with Jim Brown and Raquel Welsch, and all dealt with seeking revenge for what seemed to be a just cause, at least in the mind of the hero. Only one ended with the hero getting tired of killing everybody then packing up and going home.

Up to now, I had never killed anyone so the killing part of the movie didn't shape my future outlook but the disregard for authority seemed to stick with me. I would give proper respect in the presence of authority but once on my own I tried to go my own way regardless of what I was told. Under the strict supervision of the stockade, I didn't have any opportunity to display my new attitude but it was there nonetheless.

The stockade also introduced me to what the Brothers called Dapp. This was a style of greeting for Black men that consisted of a hand-shake combined with any number of various movements with the hand mostly, that displayed unity among the blacks. Being black and proud was a James Brown song but even more it was a new attitude for blacks everywhere to accept our heritage with pride. The military was no exception to this trend. The 70s were full of rebellion and exploration of all sorts and I was certainly primed and ready for my share of it. In the following weeks the monotony of the stockade was the only thing that was to be expected from day to day.

One day was different that caught me by surprise. The most feared and respected brother in the stockade was working in the mess hall when I received a letter from home that contained some disturbing news about my big brother Orville. He was sick in the hospital with pneumonia. I didn't react immediately to the news but during a break in the mess hall I was eating alone when I broke down, and Smitty the guy everybody feared came over and asked what was wrong. When I told him what was wrong, he truly was concerned and told me that everything would be alright. For the first time while there I saw something that I don't think anyone else in the entire stockade would have believed was in Smitty, a tender side. Every word that he said seemed to shout power or worldly wisdom. This time he didn't even try to talk like he usually did and it shocked me so much that I must have given him a look of surprise that he could read my thought. Immediately he made a comment to snap me out of my surprise and remind me of who he was. He said, in that deep voice of his, "Get Over It and Get Back to Basics Youngblood, Survival."

This was the only time while in the stockade that anyone showed weakness or compassion toward me. It was shortly after that when I received instructions to pack my stuff for transfer.

Once packed and having said my good luck and goodbyes I was walking to the gate with my Military Police escort when the guy who was the longest holdover still at the stockade came to the gate and stood alongside me with his personal belongings. He was a white guy who never said more than two words to anyone the whole time that I was there.

This time he seemed nervous and talkative. We were handcuffed together and awaiting transport to our next destination when the M.P. told us to get up and follow him.

From there we went in an M.P. car to the airport at Fort Wood where we boarded a very small twin engine airplane.

Still cuffed together we shared our information about what we were convicted of doing and where we were going. It seemed that he was caught after being A.W.O.L. for about two years from being assigned to serve in Viet Nam. This was considered to be Desertion during war time and he was on his way to do two years in Leavenworth Federal Penitentiary in Leavenworth, Kansas.

Even though President Nixon had begun to recall troops from Nam, men were still being punished for a variety of war related crimes. Many of the men that I was in the stockade with were being court-martialed. It wasn't until we started our descent from the very bumpy ride that the thought struck me that I was handcuffed to a man going to a federal prison to do hard time. My question was, am I going to the same place by mistake or is this going to be another holdover situation that could go on and on and on? My mind started wandering to all the horror stories about what goes on in those places as I started to sweat and the guy next to me seemed even more terrified than I was.

When we landed there were two vehicles to transport us to our destinations so I could breathe a little easier as we were separated and went on our way. I couldn't help feeling sorry for the white guy because for a moment I was in his shoes, at least in my mind anyway.

As I was riding to the processing center for my new home, the signs of Army pride were apparent everywhere, on the shoulder patches of all the soldiers and on almost everywhere it could be displayed the emblem of a Big Red One was seen. I was far from being Big Red One material but after processing the name of USARB became very familiar to me. It stood for United States Army Retraining Brigade.

This was Basic Training all over again because we were not allowed to wear any rank on our uniforms and we were referred to as trainees. Even though some of the guys had been sergeants, specialists, and all ranks in between, we were all busted down to E-1 the lowest rank in the Army. The uniforms we wore could only display our last names for I.D. purposes. We were only allowed to have a maximum of twenty dollars in cash on our person at any given time and any money that we would earn was put into an account to be given to us at the end of our time at USARB or forfeited if we should be sent to Leavenworth for hard time. The list of rules to follow were handed down to us at the time that we met our SDI (senior drill instructor).

Sergeant Padilla was a huge Latino man who was very cool and calm about everything he said or did and this would serve him very well among the troops because we respected leaders who were cool under fire. This didn't mean that he was weak. Quite the contrary was true of this guy and he pleaded with us to try him and see if his threats of transfer to Leavenworth were sincere or not. His company was Charlie company and I think of my fellow soldiers as Charlies devils.

Bro Dumars was chosen to be the platoon leader probably because he looked and acted like the toughest in our bunch. We had one of every kind of criminal from violent assault to scam artist who could talk you out of the air you were breathing.

These guys in Charlie company were typical of the majority of soldiers at USARB coming from all over the country and having been given what amounted to the last chance to return to active duty. Most if not all came from big cities either the projects or broken homes but all seemed to come from poverty. I was right at home.

Some of these guys were even worse than the men at the stockade of Fort Leonard Wood. Worse in the sense that they had stories about Viet Nam far more violent than I had previously heard. Stories of soldiers who killed their own commanding officers in order to avoid going into battle where they were sure to be killed. Most were there for assault of some kind on a superior officer.

Here was where a white sergeant explained the meaning behind the colors red, black, and green as it relates to African Americans. I'm fairly sure that he did this because he saw the division along racial lines being dominated by the militant Blacks, who greeted each other with the various Dapp as was used in the different parts of the world where they had been stationed before coming to U.S.A.R.B.

Blacks were very cool in everything they did. For example; since no one was allowed to speak in the mess hall, the Brothers would greet each other by knocking on the table of the Brothers as we passed on the way to our seat. This is where I was introduced to what is called Dapp. Some of the Dapp was so complex that it could take several minutes to finish all the hand slapping and gesture making that completed one type of greeting.

A man's Blackness was called into question if he didn't learn the basic Dapp of the U.S.A.R.B. Brothers. I learned a couple of the basic Dapp but never could pick-up on the Dapp called Sangria which came from Korea. It took too long to learn.

The training Brigade was divided into two parts and two separate camps that had very different rules and privileges. First a trainee was required to complete his six weeks of training in the high security barracks before being allowed to move to the minimum security barracks. There was a four week period that was required in the minimum security section, and we even had pass privileges to visit the nearby town. A third level of residence was the most severe and a last resort for trainees, that was transfer to Fort Leavenworth. The federal penitentiary full of hardened criminals that had nothing to lose and no place to go was for troublemakers.

This fact was restated every week when a class that we attended called the 12 Step program took place. Here prisoners serving life terms from Leavenworth gave lectures and testimonies about life in prison. Once when the lecturer got offended by one of the trainees who was finding something funny about what he said the lecturer said that he could kill the trainee and it wouldn't mean a thing to him. This got our attention and demanded that we listen more carefully at each session.

Now that we had been introduced to the routine of weekly training taking place some of the more peculiar personality traits of each of us became evident. For example, there was a brother who constantly practiced martial arts moves. Other obsessions were common to most of us such as wanting to find out if there really was a wild marijuana plant that grew in Kansas as we were told. Talking about how bad we wanted sex. There were many things that we discussed to break the monotony of our daily lives. The same time that martial arts was the current craze this short brother who professed to have been taught in Korea was never one to use his aggressively.

One day a white boy close to the same size as the brother we will call "Kelly" arrived and was making claims that he was trained by one of the martial arts masters of the orient. This caused a natural curiosity among the blacks and whites about which one was better than the other. After the tension and the betting had been raised, overall interests among almost everyone who even remotely knew about the situation called for an official challenge, and the two men in question were approached with incentives to publicly compete. As the big date drew near, they seemed to train and practice their own style of martial arts until the day finally arrived.

The area chosen to fight in was very large, about one third of a football field and it was located between two of the barracks where everyone could find either a window, rooftop, or some grass to sit and watch the results of weeks of bragging and betting by everybody except the two fighters.

I remember it quite clearly, as the end of our work week was drawing to a close sunset was only a couple of hours away. This Friday was set to be special because it was fight night.

Well, for some reason the fight was delayed until the next day so the tension was building to a feverish pitch and the mood of everyone was like dogs in heat.

Even the Saturday morning cartoons were full of characters fighting in the ring. Popeye and Bluto, Tom and Jerry, even Bugs Bunny and Yosemite Sam seemed to be in boxing shorts. So went the entire day until the afternoon had come and gone. Now it was early evening and the crowd began to gather around the spot where the fight was to take place and amazingly the two fighters had arrived dressed in loose fitting pants and without shirts or shoes.

Now it was beginning to look like there was going to be some action to speak of. Word spread like thunder about the fight was about to begin and the crowd gathered just as quickly to see what we had all been waiting for.

There were people lining the rooftops and hanging out of every window facing the field cheering and calling out predictions and profanities. Even the field itself was turning into a circle of people around the two fighters. As the two were stretching and moving closer to each other, they both kneeled directly across from each other and seemed to be praying when suddenly, the white boy got up and ran as fast as he could away from the field and crowd. He broke through the circle of people and vanished into one of the doors of a building.

Dead silence came over the crowd for about the length of one minute and one of the brothers shouted a name like Punk Ass White Boys, then all hell seemed to break out Blacks and Whites were fighting each other for no apparent reason. Maybe it seemed like somebody had to fight and since somebody struck the first blow then it was every man for himself.

People were running everywhere and the compound siren went off as my squad and platoon began to regroup at the barracks where we were supposed to be. This was our first reaction to the apparent riot that was in full bloom.

We could see people fighting and jumping on others outside our building but we thought that we were safe because all of the action seemed to be outside. There was only one white guy among us as we discussed the surprising turn of events of the day and we talked calmly as chaos was still ensuing outside.

Suddenly the door flew open and a line of Brothers jogged through the center of the building but as they passed by the last one to pass picked up a foot locker and threw it at the white guy hitting him square in the head. To the shock of us all, the white guy fell to the floor as the jogging Brothers vanished through the opposite door at the other end of the barracks.

As the white guy staggered to his feet bleeding and cursing he kept repeating, "What did I do?" then Bro Smith gave him a towel to place on his bleeding wound.

None of us knew why this happened but it was fairly obvious that his being white was the reason. We felt sorry for him and tried to give him some comfort until he left for the doctor, after he was gone the laughter and imitations of the incident began. I could not keep from laughing even though the actual event was certainly painful for him. One of the Brothers did his imitation of the guy getting hit and his reaction that was so funny everybody fell down in laughter.

The entire complex was now on complete lockdown. M.Ps were everywhere as the loudspeakers announced that anyone caught outside of his assigned building would be confined and charged with participating in a riot. Most of us were already expecting something like this and were standing or sitting at or near our bunk when the call to attention was given and head-count was taken. Amid the chaos those of us who were out of place were given time to return to his bunk.

Before long all was quiet but the events of the day were very fresh in everyone's head.

Even after lights-out the conversation was all about Kung-Fu vs. Jim Kelly or whatever version of the days turn of events rated further comments.

As the night passed quietly it was a good thing that this took place on a Sunday because the following day was a workday. This morning was cautiously quiet particularly due to fear of more restrictions that may be imposed if the same mood was present in the compound as was seen on Sunday.

The result of a crazy weekend was the removal of a few men both black and white who were identified as the most violent attackers of the seriously injured. Kung-Fu and Jim Kelly were left alone after that day and life returned to normal as much as possible leading up to the next phase of our retraining process. This phase would include a twenty mile forced march to the firing range where we would pitch our tents and qualify with M-16's during the night maneuvers. For weeks we had been waiting for this night because it meant that the following week transfer to a minimum security facility would be forthcoming.

If you can imagine our preparation for this march and camp out then you could vision all of our stuff that we had to pack for travel including combat gear. The weight of our backpack had to exceed 20 lbs. and we still had to add our M-16 before the march began. A canteen of water was at least 5 lbs. and the metal helmet was about 5 more, so you get the full picture of just how hard this challenge was to be even for the most physically fit soldier.

Before sunrise we were in formation and ready to leave. As we marched the drill sergeant called cadence, adding his own rhymes here and there to break the monotony and take our mind off the heat and weight of our load. The further away from the base we got, the steeper the road became. Now it seemed uphill all of the way and the trucks carrying the supplies and drill sergeant's gear drove around us to set up camp before we got there. People riding with them were injured or given special permission called a "profile" explaining the medical condition that kept them from marching with us.

Ten miles into the march we finally got a ten minute break. Even though I was a smoker this was one time that I passed on the smoke break. The air was getting thinner and we even had a few men to pass out but the march went on and the medic vehicle picked up those who needed it. The man calling cadence had long ago stopped rhyming and was only occasionally calling "yo' left, yo left, yo left right," to keep us from slowing down or bumping into each other.

The only thing that was better than reaching our destination was the breath-taking view at the top of the plateau where we would soon pitch our tents. From this point as far as you could see there was not a single man-made structure or moving vehicle in sight. It was as if God had been the only one to touch it. Directly behind us was the pathway to the firing range and the lookout towers. To the east was the mess tent where those who went ahead of us had set up the feeding line for us to grab our dinner.

After eating we had maybe three hours to pitch our tents and rest before sunset and preparation for the night firing exercises. Then we had to form up in a single file to go down the path to the firing range. With M-16 broken down shotgun style each of us had to collect our ammo and proceed to the waiting area for our turn to fire at the designated targets as they are called over the loud speaker. No light whatsoever was allowed anywhere beyond the beginning of the path to the range but the clip for our M-16 contained at least two tracer shells that lit up the path between our rifles and the targets. When the tracer would fire it was like a Star Wars weapon lighting up the firing range.

Sleeping bags and tents were being talked about like the girls we left behind as we finished up the exercises and waited to march back to our camp. None of the issues of race mattered to any of us. We were too tired to even think about someone being better than another or trying to put someone down. Kung-Fu and Jim Kelly were names that no one could even remember.

The night air was cold and as I wrapped up in my sleeping bag the morning came so quickly that I don't even remember going to sleep. All I know is somebody was yelling about formation in ten minutes and every head had better be accounted for.

After breakfast we only had 20 minutes to break camp and be ready for the march back to the facility. Everything went as planned and our hike back was just as tiresome as the one coming up the hill so the word for the day was simply, "Damn!"

The word was not only a cry of agony as we stretched our physical abilities beyond the usual limits, it also was a sigh of relief to know that the hardest part was finally over.

We had no graduation ceremony or recognition of outstanding achievements. All we knew is that we could move to a more relaxed type of confinement with a little more freedom. This freedom was to include an opportunity to visit beautiful downtown Junction City, Kansas. Rumors about this place had been circulated by various people from drill sergeants to cooks. Soon we would see for ourselves just how bad or good this place would prove to be for each one of us.

Just like basic training the dividing of troops was from company or platoon to division then came brigade and finally battalion. My platoon was "C" Charlie company but as we moved to a minimum security area all of that would change. As we marched, we would chant in response to the drill sergeant's cadence calling the name of our platoon. Somehow the Brothers never got caught up in the competitive spirit that the others would display over which company we belong to. Being Black seemed to be a company of its own that was understood to be more important than any other identity.

We finally had our day to pack our duffle bags and get lined up for the march to our new home for the next four weeks. Upon my arrival I was assigned to Bravo company. Here there were new people yet again to get to know and let know about me. As usual the Blacks did the same Dapp of their respective duty station or learned one that was a combination of a simple style mixed with one from either Germany or Korea.

Bravo company was told that we could get a pass to go to Junction City that would last until the last shuttle returned from there at 10 p.m. on Saturday or Sunday. If we didn't return in time, we would be considered to be A.W.O.L., absent without leave. This was an offense that could send us right back to the training that we came from or possibly to Leavenworth Penitentiary.

The very first Sunday that came along I found myself with a brother Thomas from Chicago who was trying to smooth talk a very unsightly prostitute into giving him free oral sex. This ordeal even though unsuccessful lasted until almost 9:30 p.m. and the last shuttle left for the base at 10:00 p.m. sharp. The taillights were growing very dim as we ran to catch the last bus and when we shouted they only got dimmer until the bus was out of sight. Because we were told to always travel in pairs this is why I stuck with Bro Thomas for so long. This proved to be a terrible mistake because the hike back to the base was at least 10 miles and if we were caught on the road after midnight, we would be accused of trying to escape. That offense is worse than even A.W.O.L. so our only option was to hike and not be seen.

As we began our off-road hike, we discussed a number of strategies for our return to go undetected but time was catching up with us as Monday morning formation and head-count would take place at 6:00 a.m.. The country road that led back seemed endless because we had to dodge headlights the whole 10-mile journey. Soon we could see sunlight starting to show signs of morning so we really had to run the rest of the way.

Out of breath and only a few minutes before head-count our plan to get inside the gate as soon as it opened without being seen by any drill sergeants or M.P.s had to be flawless or it was over for us. When the gates opened at 5:50, we had to run past the guards without being recognized so we took off our shirts and ran as fast as possible when the guard turned to go back inside the gate. This had to work because the guard could not leave his post to chase after us and that's exactly how it happened. They didn't even have time to yell STOP! before we were running through the barracks to our bunks and lockers to change. God spared us yet again from certain punishment if we had been caught. I had learned my Junction City lesson and never returned.

Minimum security was almost just like basic training except for the 12 step meetings we were required to attend where the convicted felons from Leavenworth gave their testimonies to discourage any further criminal behavior by us. Here some of the guys really tried to warn us that hard time was to be avoided at all cost. One of the other men who gave testimony told us that he was only there to get a change of scenery and he didn't give a damn whether he saw us in Leavenworth or not. This was the most convincing argument of just how heartless the inmates really were, in my opinion.

From there on I walked the straight and narrow path until my turn to leave and go to a new training station where my new skills would be taught to me. I was sent directly to Fort Jackson, South Carolina, for supply clerk training. Here I was told that there would also be females taking classes with us and after so long doing without, I was going to enjoy the change.

The change didn't seem to inspire me to become a better person because now I had a reputation to live up to as a convict and slick St. Louisan. Maybe it was peer pressure or just the idea that being a Black Man meant being like Shaft, Superfly, or Sweet Sweetback. The man my father was didn't even begin to appeal to me even though he had done some of the most heroic things that I had ever seen in my life. I saw him take a sharp butcher knife from a drunk man who tried to fight my dad in our own house and later on I saw him rescue a girl from being raped on the street right behind our house. None of these things even came to mind as I plotted to become a Robin Hood of sorts to support my marijuana smoking habit.

The plan was to seek out strangers who had bags of weed to sell and ask to check it out, then take as much as I could without a fight or getting caught. This became my profession and made me quite popular with my fellow dope smokers. Whenever we were out of money I would spring into action and let the good times roll. The way I was so successful was to choose people who I didn't know from a unit far from our own.

The first time was the easiest but it got riskier every time after that either for me or the person who told me where to find my victim. God showed me how it felt to be tricked once when I was shooting dice and got completely cleaned out before figuring out that I had been playing with loaded dice. Even that didn't stop me from my life of crime. I continued to believe that I was somehow doing a good thing by taking dope from dealers and getting my friends and myself high.

AMAZING GRACE

During this time heroes of every kind were appearing on the silver screen and all of them were doing whatever they wanted to "Get Over." My life was becoming a movie that I was starring in. The parts I didn't like would be cut and the good stuff replayed for friends later. Now came the part when the girl who guys were looking at shows some interest in me and I go on the attack.

Marie was somewhat shy but fully able to hold her own with any man's conversation or gameplan. I found her to be very interesting and sisterlike as I had my eye on better things. This is where my strategy had to be different from the hundreds of other guys in the running for her affections, so I boldly promised to come to her room before I left the base if she would give me some when I did. Surprisingly she said yes, but knowing the failure rate and severe penalty for getting caught doing such a thing I'm sure that she thought I couldn't possibly be serious.

As my date to leave grew closer and closer, I would remind her that I was serious and to expect me on the night before I was leaving. She kept on teasing me with playful answers to my questions about which window was hers and will her roommate give us time alone when I made it. By this time, I had already mapped out the route to the window and timed the gap between the passing of the guards. Here again my movie heroes had played a major role in the planning of this mission. Bruce Lee,

James Bond, and T.H.E. Cat had already shown me how to move in the shadows and wear black from head to toe.

This was the big night and I was ready with my black hush-puppies and all black turtle-neck beneath my black skull-cap. At the stroke of midnight while all were asleep and the time was perfect for guard duty change, I crept from bush to bush just as my plan was until I reached the perimeter of the ladies' barracks where no man was allowed unless facing court martial and jail time. Past the point of no return, I continued as planned with heart pounding and sweating through my cat burglar gear until I reached the corner that was my climbing point to the second floor where my reward awaited my arrival. The second that the guards passed each other I climbed the gutter pipe to the flat metal awning beneath the second floor and lay flat while they passed once again.

Now I was at the window of my promised land, so I knocked lightly until someone came and opened the window but it was not Marie so I asked if she was there and the girl said she was on fireguard duty in the hall. The young lady went to get her while I lie flat again until she returned with Marie who was in total shock but still willing to kiss me and tell me that she thought I was playing and couldn't let me in under the circumstances, so I said okay and slowly made my way back to my own territory without getting caught. Little did I know that for years after that adventure Marie would stay in touch with me through my parents address and phone number that I gave her.

The next morning I was on a flight home for 10 days of leave before going to my next duty station. All of my friends were working during the day and at night I was on my own if they had to get up for work the next day. All of this free time found me at Northwest Plaza shopping one day when I saw a woman right out of the fashion magazines she must have been at lunch from her job in the plaza and I couldn't resist asking her what time she got off of work. Upon asking her if I could give her a ride home, she said yes and I fell head over heels for Terri who lived in Northwoods. We spent most of my time together and I was hooked. She had a baby son whom I got along with and I saw a future with her. We spent all of my time together when I came home and even went to the Kansas City "Kool Jazz Festival" in the summer of 1973. I helped her pick out a little red compact car to drive to and from work but it was a stick shift so I also had to teach her to drive a stick. Much of the time when I came over to her house, I was high and must have displayed signs of being that way even to her parents whom I respected and tried to impress most of the time. She had a big family and they lived in a big house that seemed peaceful and unified under the leadership of her father, a friendly but serious man as I can recall. Her younger brother was a bit different because he must have thought I was not a real soldier. He would always challenge me in one way or another until one day that changed his view of me.

One evening as Terri and I talked outside in the street, she was sitting on a slight hill while I stood facing her in the street. Her brother came from out of nowhere and Kung-Fu kicked me in the back right into the hill where Terri was sitting. My only thought was the cartoon of Bugs Bunny and his famous quote, "As you may realize, this means war."

While picking myself up, I could see that this young man had removed his shoes and was prepared to continue kicking me as long as I would let him, so I removed my shoes and bounced over to the middle of the street where he waited for me. Like most young men who were fans of Bruce Lee, I had been practicing several kicks and moves from the master and while it was obvious that her brother was comfortable with the side kick, I had other plans. After giving him two or three clean kicks directly into my shoulder I timed his next kick perfectly and did a roundhouse kick that would have caught him square in the face if I hadn't restrained myself at the moment of impact. He fell to the ground as if I had hit him but was so shocked at the power of what could have been that he was finished and totally embarrassed at the same time.

I tried to come home every weekend just to spend some time with Terri and her son as we grew closer and closer. If not for my immaturity and stubbornness we might have been together for a long time but as fate would have it I made a huge mistake one weekend as I sat in her parents' family room.

I was watching a male ballet dancer on T.V. at her parents' house with the entire family and when everyone had been commenting about how graceful and talented the guy looked, I was asked what I thought. I must have looked as high as I really was and all eyes turned to me when I said that the guy looked like a "punk" to me. Terri grabbed me by the arm and marched me to the door where she told me I had to leave. I tried to apologize later but Terri was done with me. Broken hearted, I had to move on.

My orders were to report to Fort Campbell, Kentucky, home of the Airborne Infantry Screaming Eagles where Jump school was always encouraged for the $55 extra on your paycheck each jump you made monthly. My dear parents allowed me to drive all of the way to Fort Campbell in the near new Buick LeSabre that my father had been driving so I was all ready to take the Fort by storm.

Here is where my journey gets interesting because now I got to have a regular job and people to work with instead of training. My commanding officer's name was Captain Jones, an easy name to remember but like metal to a magnet I found my way to the wild bunch. Names like Dirty Red, O.D. Juice Jones, who by the way was known for his alcoholic tendencies, were just a few of the characters that crossed my path. Because people still found common ground in what was called "HOMIES" the people from St. Louis got together and talked about mutually visited spots and widely known local topics concerning St. Louis.

Dirty Red, nicknamed for his light skinned complexion, red hair, and willingness to fight dirty was from East St. Louis and tried to live up to his area's reputation for being street schooled and careless. O.D. was a white boy from the west coast who was known for his variety of drugs that he constantly took or sold on a daily basis, but Juice Jones was memorable as well because he always had a half pint of something within reach to turn up and drink as if it were Kool-Aid. Juice was an older soldier who had been a sergeant nearing the end of his service from Nashville a fairly large city only 50 miles away from Fort Campbell. These characters stood out at the beginning but every couple of months someone new would take the cake all over again. Whenever someone got orders to leave there would be a replacement to fill their spot soon after the move.

It was mid-October when I arrived with my own car and I must believe that Dirty Red attached himself to me more for my transportation than for our mutual St. Louis connection. Nevertheless, we started hanging out together and he tried to show me some of the ropes as he knew them to be. Here is where I found out that Chapman's (Dirty Red's) real name was Fanton Chapman a surprisingly different name for a simply drug driven person, as he was, who looked for action of only two kinds money and women. Drugs were just a part of everyday life to start the day looking for a high stay high all day and end the day getting high as well.

Our game was only good as long as we were high enough to think our rapp was stronger than it really was. The truth is that all of our rapp came from one of the latest soul artists or another, since we bought all of the music that we could get from every body's hometown music source. Every night we would gather in someone's bunkbed space and get wasted before crashing like an aircraft on fire. Whoever had a boombox playing a new cassette would likely be the host of the evening drug fest. Those who didn't get high would find something else to do or place to go until things died down and they always did. Once the party reached a certain point everyone would kinda cool down and eventually go to sleep.

My MOS was 71B30 which meant that I had successfully typed a total of 30 words per minute during my training. This was true and with some time I could have been able to do it again but this however, was not the time to ask me to do it. When I reported for duty, this was exactly what was expected of me along with properly typing military correspondence to be sent to high-ranking officers in the HHB DIVARTY section where I was assigned. The letters stood for Headquarters Battery Division Artillery a place where a whole lot of saluting and standing at attention was the daily order of business. A brother from L.A. named Kenneth Askew was my immediate superior who tried to help me get back in the groove of typing but at this point I was expected to know the proper format of various Department of Defense letter writing. My gap in time from getting certified as a Clerk-Typist and serving my time in retraining was too long for me to remember how to write those letters so I was soon reassigned to my secondary MOS, the supply room where stocking became my daily job.

For reasons that didn't matter then and still don't matter St. Louis homeys would get together to find rides home on payday weekends. Life was beginning to seem normal. Typing letters for officers to send to each other and orders for personnel was getting the best of me and my superiors could see that I wasn't performing at the necessary level to maintain my position so I was shuffled around to see where I fit in. Finally, I found a comfortable fit as a Field Wireman running wire for communication between stations where units were camped out in the field.

The devil seems to find us whenever we are proud and impatient. As I went about my travels with Chapman we went to a nightclub called the E.M. (enlisted men's) club where I ran into one of the brothers from my time at the retraining brigade who Satan must have hand picked. He had been there a little while longer than me and had connections in Hopkinsville where he convinced me to drive my car for some fun. This meant drugs, women, and gambling for big bucks. These were things that I was too proud to deny that I was interested in. Next came the chance to make some fast money by robbing the big time gambler at the crap house, and I was too impatient to pass what seemed a fool proof plan for robbing him. All of these plans and even the gun to rob him with came by way of my good friend from U.S.A.R.B. and our confinement in Kansas.

At this time I was hanging out with a brother from the Big Apple (New York) by the name of Isaac Polite, a cool guy who had wit intelligence and still was a bit humble in his own way. Ike was so cool that he could win an argument without saying a word, or make me laugh just by a look that he would give me. We would go almost everywhere together and tried to enjoy any points of interest we could find in my '72 LeSabre so this night was no different. Ike and I were roaddoggs on this night taking on any and all adventures that came along. When the idea to rob the crap game came up our friend who suggested the crime gave all kinds of excuses why he couldn't be the one to do it. He took us to get high at one of his friends' apartments in Hoptown and he gave the same excuses as to why he couldn't be the one either. Once we got high enough smoking hash from Germany, Ike and I could see that the obvious best candidates for the job was us.

The plan was simple enough, one of us would put the gun to the guy's head and the other one of us would knock him out with a jack handle. We were given a nickel plated snubnose .38 to use in the robbery and it reminded me of one of the many guns that my father had in his collection. At first Ike and I were arguing over who would use the gun and who would knock the guy out but my experience with pistols gave me the upper hand and Ike gave in rather quickly to the idea of me being the trigger man. Ike even talked about how he had knocked out this guy in New York and had no problem doing it again, especially for a cut of over $2000 as we were being told that this guy was winning. There was a girl at the crap game watching how much this guy was winning and calling us to tell us how his luck was running. At this point he was over $2k and climbing. We got into my car and headed out on the highway where my partner test fired the pistol out the window of the car. At this point we felt like we could do anything.

When we arrived at the apartment building where the game was, we had already said that someone would hang out the window upstairs and signal when the guy was coming down the steps so I could pretend to be going inside as he was coming out and put an armlock on him as I put the gun to his head. The very next thing to happen was for Ike to knock the guy out, and the rest would be easy.

As we got out of the car and stood around the front of the building our inside man went upstairs and got his position at the window. Ike and I smoked a cigarette and waited for the signal that our guy was coming. Suddenly it happened and we sprung into action, me at the front of the door and Ike behind it when the door began to open and I automatically started to walk as if I was coming into the door while our victim was coming out.

My left arm hooked his and my right hand and arm hooked his while I put the gun to his head. At this point he was in shock and fear as he threw his hands into the air signaling his full surrender. Here is where Ike could have knocked him out with the jack handle as planned but as in all perfect plans this one wasn't so perfect. As I held our victim at bay something very strange happened.

When the door closed to reveal Ike standing behind it with the jack handle in hand he was face to face with our victim as I held him in an armlock with the gun to his head. This must have been too much for Ike because he froze in his tracks and fell backwards like Fred Sanford having one of his heart attacks that he called the "Big One." Nothing was being said by anyone at this time because I was in as much shock about the turn of events as our victim was. It seemed like a long time was passing with only silence and nothing else even after Ike had dropped the jack handle and ran away. So much time had passed that I had time to think about what my next move should be. Should I shoot the guy or maybe remove the gun and say, "Awe man, we was just playing," then try to walk away. Because I didn't know the guy nor him know me, neither option made a lot of sense.

Here is where things got kinda crazy. The victim must have gotten tired of this gun pressing against his head and decided to find out if it was loaded or maybe if he could take it away from me and save himself. He grabbed for the gun and almost got it but when he did it became obvious that I had no intention of killing him for his money because I pointed the gun into the air while we fought over it. As I tried to push him away, he seemed determined to hold on to both my hand and any piece of the gun that he could touch. We fell off the porch onto a parked car still fighting over who would get the better grip on the gun until I could see that he was getting close to having a better grip than I did on the gun. My only chance seemed to be to toss the gun and run, so I did and as he turned to get the gun, I kicked him hard enough to keep him off balance while I ran for cover around the side of the building.

Most of the evening it had been raining and the ground was soaked and muddy so as I ran it felt like I was not getting nearly enough traction for the effort that I was putting into this run for my life. By the time I reached the corner of the building he was aiming at me and his first shot took a chip out of the brick in the wall when I ran around the corner to the back. Just as I slipped in the mud while running around the side of the apartments, I thought I would fall for sure because my feet left the ground completely but I knew that I couldn't or it would mean certain death. My feet slipped out from under me, but somehow I kept upright and found myself continuing to run all of the way around the back of the building as I searched for more secure cover. Just then he came behind me still shooting at me as I ran. There was one bullet that spun and flew past my right ear so close that I could hear it as it went passed my head. It sounded like a bee flying at supersonic speed. The guy who was chasing me slipped in the exact spot where I had almost fallen only a second before but he went down and gave me time to get to another apartment building where I quickly closed the door behind me.

Still in panic mode I looked for an open door that I could go into and possibly use the back door or window to complete my escape. People must have heard the shots and saw me running toward their building because I could hear doors slamming and locks clicking as soon as I entered the apartment stairway. There were only four doors in the area of the spiral staircase and as the last one at the top of the stairs was slowly closing, I ran and put my foot in the door at the very last second.

Pushing my way through the door a teenaged black boy was the one trying to close the door when I entered and shut the door behind me. He was shocked at my boldness upon entry but as I tried to lie as fast as I could a second passed when I could see the rest of the room. This was the living room and the entire family must have been in here watching TV. A color console was against the wall to the right of the door and in the middle of the room sat a very elderly black woman who seemed to be undisturbed by any of the activity either inside or out. Two small children were sitting directly in front of the TV on the floor and they seemed excited about what was on the TV. As fast as I could talk, I started asking questions about was there a gun in the house and if there was a back door even as I told my lie about being chased by a jealous boyfriend of a girl I was visiting.

As I listened for the front door of the building to open, talking and looking around at the same time a thought struck me that helped to calm me down. Maybe this guy who was chasing me was not very anxious to open another door that he didn't know what was behind it. Maybe he wouldn't come any further to get me especially seeing how he has my gun and I have nothing of his. At this point I got the nerve to peep out the window and I could see him heading away from the parking lot and getting into another car to leave. This was my chance to thank the family who had not kicked me out as they should have and leave the area before the police arrived.

My thank yous were short but nonetheless sincere. As I exited the building and made my way to my car, I saw Ike and he couldn't believe that I wasn't shot or dead. All he could do was repeatedly say how shocked he was that I was alive. We immediately left the area as we could see police cars coming to the building where the incident first occurred. Slowly we drove away as if we were unaware of the reason the police were called.

After all that had happened, I should have been humbled by God's grace in saving my life but I was feeling proud and even more bold than ever. At this point I was over the edge, no one could tell me anything. I decided to purchase my own gun and start packing just in case I ran into the guy I tried to rob again. My best friend Ike began to distance himself from me and I would find myself with guys from other platoons around the base. Having a car may not have been the best thing as I traveled back and forth to Hoptown and Clarksville looking for action.

Weeks had passed when I wouldn't call home or even think of going home until one night after a night of drugs, sex, and partying my new roaddog said that he had spied out a service station where he wanted to do something and I drove around back while he went inside. When I drove 'round front and picked him up he ran and got in and we drove off but someone inside was calling and looking at us as we drove off. Seconds later police swooped down on us and arrested us for armed robbery.

My first and only phone call was to my father's house. As I sat in what resembled the dungeons of the ancient Roman empire my thoughts were racing back and forth on the many ways that I should have avoided this terrible fate that lies ahead. For two days I couldn't sleep afraid that a rat or giant bug would bite me if I did. Finally, we were moved to the county jail which was at least a little bit cleaner but much smaller fitting four men into a space the size of a large closet and a toilet seat in the center of the room. My roaddog and I began to get very acquainted with each other since we didn't really know each other before going on this free-for-all night of hell raising.

His name was Lloyd from Chicago and a pretty good home as he described it. The other two guys were from the immediate area and just plain thieves and angry men who couldn't stay out of trouble. There was a common area where a small table was for the people from three cells could go in the morning if they chose to stay out there all day until time to eat came later in the afternoon.

This was home for two weeks until my father came to bail me out at my arraignment. He was accompanied by his friend Mr. Frank McComb who had known me since I was a baby. When my name was called for release, I didn't know how to act, sad for those left behind or just overjoyed that I was getting out. It was the dead of winter and when I got to the car with Daddy I hugged and thanked him but we immediately loaded into the car and began driving toward home. Snow was falling faster than I had seen it fall before and the heavy Buick Deuce and a quarter had to plow through many drifts as we made our way in what became 24 inches of snow before we finally got home. It took us over nine hours to drive a five-hour distance through the snow. Seeing the gateway arch was about the most exciting thing that I had ever seen after having doubts about even seeing home again.

My mother was tending bar when my father had me go inside and tell her that I was home. She ran from behind the bar and gave me the biggest hug that she ever has even since that time until now. Sleeping in my old bed was better than it had ever been before and Mom's food never tasted better either. You would think that I'd change my entire life around but silly me was right back where I started looking for sex, drugs, and the party.

I was still considered a soldier so I had to return to Fort Campbell and try to finish my enlistment term. For the most part I followed the rules and stayed out of trouble but that didn't mean that I stopped smoking weed or partying even though my father took back the vehicle that I had been using to get into so much trouble. On weekends I would still try to get home with my homeys Bro Jolley, Herb, Smiley, and Herb's cousin, Eric. When I could get a ride with someone I would, even if it meant bringing someone who was from another city with me to visit. Bro Kenneth Mims from Texas had bought a '62 Chevy Malibu with several mechanical issues but we made the trip at least twice with only minor repairs along the road on our five-hour trip.

None of the vehicles that were purchased near the Fort came with warranties or cost much more than $500 at the time so the average age of most of the rides that took us to and from St. Louis was always at least ten years or older. The best trips I recall making would have to be the ones in Herb's old Cadillac when I could sink into the back seat and sleep comfortably for the whole five hours.

On the other hand, one trip back to the base in Eric's Dodge posed a couple of serious challenges. Besides having a full load of six people I had to ride in what was known as the "Bitch's" spot in the middle of the front seat. In Eric's Dodge this meant that for the entire five hours I would be squeezed between the driver and the passenger in front but in addition to riding the middle hump I had to avoid touching or kicking Eric's self-installed 8 track tape player located directly in front of my feet.

At first this didn't seem so hard but my legs got so tired of the position I was in that one of them slipped off of the hump and hit the wires for the 8 track.

Immediately all of the headlights, taillights, windshield wipers, and interior electric shut down and Eric was driving 80 mph blind in the rain on a deserted highway for about 30 seconds until he stopped on the side of the road. As we came to a stop in total darkness at about 1 a.m. we could see an 18 wheeler's headlights coming our way and hear his bullhorn blowing as he flew past our disabled Dodge. Since Eric put the 8 track in himself and had an extra fuse he was able to repair the short and get us back on the road with his flashlight in hand.

From there on I had to keep my feet on the passenger side of the hump while being smacked on the backside of my head and called various kinds of M F's. This would have been scary enough, but as we traveled further in the rain we could see a bridge far ahead that ascended above the river as we could also see clearly. Everyone including our driver, Eric, was getting a little sleepy but as Eric sped to the bridge's entrance the road vanished under a sheet of water that was part of the river we were supposed to be crossing. The water splashed up on both sides of the Dodge with a loud spraying echo as we pushed ahead to more highway and the bridge itself, but by now we all had been shocked into total awareness of the water surrounding us below the bridge we were now crossing and our main concern was what is coming up on the other side.

Eric cautiously approached the end of the bridge before we all realized that higher ground was ahead and the river bank would stop the rising water from reaching the highway. We continued on the highway until reaching our final gas stop near Hopkinsville. Safely back on the base, we all thanked God for keeping us from disaster and I stayed on the grounds for a few weekends and fought the boredom with friends who couldn't go home either. At a low point one weekend, my roaddog Ike and

I had been noticing that one of the white guys who didn't mingle very much left his orange and white Chevy Camaro parked right between two of the barracks. We thought it was a nice car and we walked past from the mess hall to also notice that it wasn't locked. The only other question that needed answering was, did the owner leave the keys in it.

I got inside and looked around under the seat and in the glove box but no keys were to be found so Ike and I just got inside to pretend that we were going somewhere. While playing like I was driving I turned the ignition keyhole and to our utter surprise the car started and purred with the hum of a race car. Gas was already in the tank so Ike and I changed our clothes and cruised the base for available passengers. We didn't find any women but a Puerto Rican friend of Ike's offered to buy gas for a trip to Nashville, 50 miles away, so off we went. The sight-seeing trip was very relaxing and we came back renewed and ready to tackle the next week.

After coming home frequently on weekends when I wasn't confined to the base for one reason or another, I was discharged under Honorable conditions and came back to Kinloch and my parents' house. This began my new and improved view of Kinloch and our neighbors. My dad had won the office of Alderman in his ward and the school district was being dismantled with the students going to the newly formed Ferguson-Florissant school district. The smaller towns that were part of this new district had little or no say so about the operations or curriculum being offered. Bussing had become the way to go to school from the government desegregation law. Even then plans to destroy Kinloch's way of life were taking effect. There were schools in every city around us but none in our abandoned buildings. I was still as wild as ever so my goals were still the same as they were when I was in the military. The only difference was that I didn't want anything to do with law breaking or jail and my classmates still saw me as one of them.

Wonder Years

When I left, I was a senior at Kinloch High so to this day my classmates still allow me the privilege of being called one of the graduating class of '73. That title carried with it a greater sense of maturity than I should have been allowed to claim so I tried to be a better man as the years passed.

Coming home presented certain challenges like needing a job, living with parents, and still smoking weed. Being a vet had its advantages and after a short vacation of unemployment insurance the summer offered a job for me at the St. Louis County Department of Planning. Here was a summer job driving my own vehicle throughout the county verifying addresses and assigning them an individual locator number to be used for the new computerized data system at County Headquarters.

The job was perfect for me in every way. I got to drive around town with a beautiful Sista from U-City who wrote down numbers as we read the addresses on each apartment building. The one problem that kept coming up was white people who called police on us as we did our job and my boss having to verify my need to be where I was while I was handcuffed. This used to happen in the white neighborhoods but never in Black communities even as we did our job the exact same way all of the time.

As the summer came to an end and the job ended too, a former girlfriend and I began to see each other. She got pregnant and we continued to stay together for the rest of the year.

When I was about to become a father, I married Glenda the same girl who I was introduced to years earlier at Gloria's home. We moved into the Belue-Hadnot apartments (the projects) right across the street from Hal's Drive-in burger joint.

Only 12 years after the riot of '62 Hal's was still the meeting spot for people traveling up or down Kinloch's main road, now renamed MLK Drive. Living in the projects was not bad considering the opportunities that it presented. The bus ran right past the front door, city hall was across the street, and the rent was only 30% of the household income. My dad was able to put in a good word for me at his factory job, and on the day my first baby girl was born, I got my first paycheck from the automotive parts manufacturing job where he had worked for many years.

Becoming a father changed the most basic instinct I had been following all of my life to put my own desires first at all times. Marriage had been a selfish act because it wasn't done out of a devotion to be faithful to my wife but to maximize my access to tax benefits. Holding in my arms the most precious gift God could entrust to my care cut through every layer of vanity and selfish desire that was in me. Katrina became my pride and joy, but Mary Jane had become too strong a force in my life to be ignored. Smoking cigarettes was bad enough but marijuana added the formula for financial fog that clouded most of my daily decisions about what direction to take.

My honorable discharge allowed me to receive a financial benefit for going to college, so I was all over that but didn't focus on any trade other than journalism. My part-time student status allowed me to acquire an Associate's Degree and a monthly government check to pay for tuition but would that be enough to succeed or not.

Before I knew that Kinloch was an Irish name, my first belief was that everybody was "Kin" to each other but were "locked" in the same living area and space thus the name Kinloch. I also spelled it with a "k" at the end.

As a young journalism student in the 80s I needed to talk to someone who lived and grew old in Kinloch from it's beginning to see if there was anything special making the people different or better. A person who rose above all expectations and demanded the respect she deserved as an educator from her students first then her peers. She demanded it with the way she walked, talked, and carried herself as a woman of over 90 years who seemed as royal as the queen of England. She was elegant and proper but knew how to sound just like my mother when she told me to, "Sit your butt down, boy." For a moment I was able to see why her name was feared by grade school kids as I grew up. Then she sat at her kitchen table with coffee in hand to let me interview her. The gems she shared were found more in the experience of speaking with her in her home than the notes I was able to take.

Human contact with others has proven to be the most historic events ever to take place as proven by our divine creator Himself so my desire is to both make my readers cry and laugh out loud as I have done in writing about my contacts with many unforgettable *people* who lived next door to Ferguson.

I was told by the woman commonly known as the first baby born in Kinloch about its beginnings and how her father came there in a horse drawn wagon to a place known for horse racing stables and the need for laborers to care for that industries property. Former slaves who bet on a new way of life could occasionally forget about many of the evils of racism while proving themselves valuable to each other and then the world. That's what seed was planted by the Bragg family in Kinloch where Etta and Ruth were born.

Mrs. Etta Hill told me most of what I know about Kinloch's beginning and who was there, the rest came from my people and my own experiences growing up "Next Door to Ferguson."

Mrs. Hill started by telling me Sheriff Bracey became the first Black lawman in Kinloch and it's not clear who gave him his badge or authority but keeping the peace was simply the name given to keeping things quiet in what amounted to the "Black Dodge City" of middle America. When people got along life could be beautiful, but when trouble started anything was possible and didn't always get handled quietly. Many of the Black cowboys were being handled by beautiful Black women while these proud Black Cowboys were handling race horses for breeders nearby. For most early residents settling down and raising families became more important than wild living or drifting wherever the wind blew. As word spread that Blacks were quietly living in this little town, the population slowly grew. Even if it meant a bit of a struggle the idea of a peaceful existence was worth the effort. Cousins and relatives on every level heard about a place to go without so many of the white man's hoops to jump through. Opportunity seemed to be available and very little was needed to start. Many of Kinloch's people came directly from East St. Louis after a horrible massacre took place there that devastated the Black owned industry and families.

Blacks from everywhere needed to regroup and reset from the "Red Summer" of 1920 and 21. This was the time when white people who had been considered poor and middle class all across the country began to use fear of Black Veterans from WWI as an excuse to wage war on Black communities. This was a time when brave veterans banded together in the nation's capital to protect their families from white terrorists. White folk also feared the Great Migration from the South which was in full swing. They feared the possibility that Blacks were taking jobs from white people and working for less too.

Families looking for people like themselves who just wanted to live the American dream in peace came here. Mrs. Hill pointed out how notorious Black outlaws would hide out in plain sight of the law and even in some cases make a new respectable life for themselves in Kinloch.

The landscape being uneven, hilly, and generally unpaved made the area known as Kinloch today undesirable to most white people so we were thought of as poor and unable to do any better. Kinloch's riches could be found in the people who chose to live there. People who found a way to respect themselves and their neighbors in spite of the cultural differences that existed from house to house they all had a common history of being Black.

Almost everyone had to make a living somewhere else in St. Louis but come home and raise kids as they made the best of their situation, whatever that called for. The educated didn't look down on the uneducated because they all dealt with the same racial stumbling blocks at the end of the day. Those who knew how to lead were even encouraged to organize by visionary neighbors who at the time lacked the formal education needed to match their survival skills but knew the value of what they had acquired on the battlefield of life.

Kinloch's incorporation in the 1930s right after the Great Depression gave birth to the political concept of self-government for Blacks and recognition in the areas of education and business management. Scratching and clawing to grow from a one room school house to a board of education was a huge part of Kinloch's institution building struggle. Mrs. Etta Hill said that they had to march and protest just to have schools built before incorporation. She didn't want to talk about her husband or the fact that they didn't have any children so I didn't push the issue, but her very light complexion had to be part of the story she could have told because her educational accomplishments were rare for people of color at that time. She could and probably did pass for white in order to reach the level of respect that she brought with her to Kinloch's Dunbar Elementary School.

Her huge house and yard were constantly patrolled by at least one Doberman Pincher and one or two Boxers unless Mr. James called them to the gated dog pen where he would put them when I came over. The house looked like a fenced history museum but once inside it felt like a place anyone would love to call home. Entering from the south were a few concrete steps then the breakfast room before reaching the next step up and the black and white color coordinated kitchen where tiles on the floor matched the smaller ceramic tiles on the walls. Through the next door they had a grand piano in the living room and a wall of books and antique furniture from a period before I was born. At the north end was a screened in sitting room that must have doubled as a front porch in the summer months. I learned early on not to even try to visit without an invitation or phone call before showing up. Mrs. Hill lived with her sister Ruth and Ruth's husband, Mr. James Short. They each had stories of their own but they needed time before opening that gateway. We knew at an early age not to get too close to the fence while the dogs were loose, so I treated the family history the same way.

A grand piano in the sitting room suggested someone had a musical background and it was no surprise to find out in my later years that Miss Ruth had made a name for herself in the entertainment industry. Her slightly darker complexion didn't allow her to pass for white so despite her heavy make-up that she wore, an obvious difference separated the sisters' personality composition. Miss Hill was reserved and didn't go out for recreational events much but I can recall Miss Ruth being the life of many of my parents' house parties and bar-b-ques.

Miss Ruth and her husband always brought their own bottle to the party but seldom brought homemade dishes like most other women were known to do. When Miss Hill and Miss Ruth were both in attendance at a social event, I clearly remember Miss Ruth smelling of alcohol and tobacco but never even a hint of it would be on Miss Hill. Mr. James Short was considered to be a hard-working husband to Miss Ruth and a fun loving neighbor to the rest of us because he loved his toys like the speedboat that he would take to Creve Couer Lake every summer. He would take us for rides on the lake but his humor reflected the fact that he never had children of his own. The financial prosperity of that childless household was no surprise either because they cared for the possessions like precious children. Even the family pets were mostly security for the property that they owned as well as guarding anything on the inside from theft.

My older sister regarded Miss Hill as a strict but fair principal of Dunbar Elementary and I believe that she truly cared for her students as her own family. Miss Hill needed to set an example for them at all times but she needed to prepare them for the real and cruel world that lay ahead.

My own struggles with family and schooling got in the way of a really deep look at her life story before she died, so what I'm left with is the memory of a close neighbor and friend. Her passing in her mid-90s was not a shock, but she was mourned just the same on the scale of the "Notorious RBG." Justice Ginsburg and Mrs. Hill could have been sisters if they were compared by physical looks in their old age and quite possibly in their younger days. A more experienced journalist would have surely taken better advantage of the wealth of knowledge to be gained from interviewing Mrs. Etta Hill, but I am grateful for what she shared.

History of Kinloch would not make sense without including people like Mrs. Hill and there were so many more characters that made life interesting I believe patches of material are missing from a beautiful quilt because the names of people who were present daily on the streets are not celebrated and remembered.

LION

One family at a time, the town grew in population and prosperity then my family name was added to the census.

My grandparents settled in Kinloch and raised my father to deal with wild neighbors at an early age because he had his own wild side that was somehow passed down to me. There must have been a lot that happened early on in my parents' lives but my father wouldn't speak of it. I found out about most of it by overhearing stories as they began to get older plus putting 2 and 2 together from memory and family talk.

Nightclubs, pool halls, liquor stores were springing up all over town and the numbers game was available to anyone with a dollar to spare and a few lucky numbers to play. Names like Tina Turner and Chuck Berry were no stranger to this night life and neither was some of America's most wanted Black gangsters who hid out in plain sight for years. Mr. McKnight had to be one of them because he owned property and businesses all over town. The numbers game was his and he drove the biggest two-toned super clean 1957 Cadillac that I have seen to this day. Kinloch must have been especially good to him or he came there with money to burn because he sure kept plenty of it in his pockets.

Mr. McKnight had a grocery/liquor store plus a tavern where the basement was being rented out to Mr. Bradfield for his barber shop where Mr. Johnson used a second chair to cut hair and talk about everybody's business who stepped through the door.

There were not many men that my father reacted to like he did Mr. McKnight. A level of respect was afforded to him even as my father only called him by his last name, "McKnight."

My family prospered and grew in many ways from opportunities afforded by Kinloch's existence but not like Mr. McKnight. He was far ahead of his time and a survivor by "Any Means Necessary." In my humble opinion, Mr. McKnight had to be some bad ass gangster who knew how to hide in plain sight. It took me almost 40 years to reach a relationship with my father that allowed us to talk about our past with each other. He knew all about mine but he was almost a total mystery to me until he started to get sick, even then the only way I suspected that my father had followed in Mr. McKnight's footsteps was when my adult cousin (Richard) called him the Godfather of Kinloch. Most of what he shared was stuff that happened after I was born but I was able to piece together some of what he was deliberately leaving out. I had one family member that no one else could come close to for my affection and that was my father's mother. As kids she was there whenever Momma or Daddy wasn't.

Before she started to get too old to share about my dad, I was too young to see the wealth of information that was hidden away in that beautiful grey head of hair.

The laid-back approach to living was taking its toll on all of my dreams of being a successful businessman and writer. Going to work every day and getting high every night began to blind me to the most important things going on around me.

One night after work the usual cars filled the diagonal parking spaces across the street from city hall all of the way down to the corner directly across from Hal's where we lived.

This was where most of the dope dealers would sit in their cars and wait for customers to come looking for them and the bomb weed they were peddling. As risky as it was to stay in one spot for too long, this allowed the dealer to drive away when police showed too much interest in the traffic coming and going. My apartment sometimes served as a quick place to be visiting when people I knew had been parked in one spot for too long and needed to look like they were visiting a resident of the immediate vicinity. John Davis was one of my best friend's older brother who was allowed to visit my home at times when he felt the need to be outside of his vehicle, like a resident would be rather than one of the dealers that police might stop and search.

On this particular night around midnight, John had invited me to sit with him in his 1968 black and white Lincoln Town Car with suicide doors to smoke a joint of the weed that he was selling. As we sat there making small talk and commenting on the potency of his product, we both noticed smoke rising from the rear of one of the apartments. John jokingly said, "Somebody barbecuing this late is making me hungry." Neither of us took the time to actually walk or even drive to see what was being done behind the apartment so he went to grab a bite and I went inside my apartment only six doors down from where we saw the smoke and went to bed.

Later that night I was awakened by the sound of sirens and people talking when I heard my wife crying right outside the front door. Going down the stairs I was met by Glenda crying and telling me, "Those babies dead." I had to see what she was talking about so I went outside and only two steps in front of the building I could see fire trucks, policemen, and an ambulance where John and I had been parked only one hour earlier. When I walked closer, I could see that the barbecue was really the early stage of what was now a raging house fire. Flames were shooting up to 20 feet high as the firemen sprayed water at them but that wasn't the greatest tragedy.

Weaving through the crowd I reached a point where I could see the lifeless bodies of three children who apparently died in the fire. They were still wearing underwear and pajamas before the firemen covered their bodies with blankets. A sadness came over me like I'd never felt before. It took quite a long time to get those images out of my head and even longer to accept the fact that I could have saved them. I don't think John ever knew the cost of our indifference and I was too ashamed to mention it to anyone for years after it happened.

Three years later Glenda had our second child, who we named after my grandmother Sophia. All seemed well when we brought her home but soon after she had been at home with us, she stopped having bowel movements and started crying non-stop until we took her to the hospital. But they couldn't figure out what was wrong with her. For an entire week we kept going to different hospitals and no one knew what was wrong. Glenda would walk the floor with Sophia as she cried and cried all day and into the night occasionally screaming in pain like a person being tortured. One night when Glenda had been trying to comfort her all day, cook, and take care of Katrina while I was at work, she was so exhausted when I got home that she almost passed out. When I got home, I took Sophia in my arms and walked the floor with her from midnight until sunrise non-stop, praying and talking to Sophia asking her, "What's wrong, Baby?" over and over as we walked a path in the floor of our bedroom. She finally went to sleep for a brief time until the pain would awaken her again. I slept while she did until I had to go to work again.

When I returned home from work that night there was a strange silence in the house, and I didn't know what to think at first. Fears of all kinds were running through my mind until Glenda came down the stairs and told me about the angel of God she met at the store who told her to try a suppository for babies and change Sophia's formula to one without iron. I went upstairs and saw what I had been praying for, my babies sleeping peacefully in bed. Now I could finally get some rest.

As soon as I had saved enough money, we moved to Berkeley but Kinloch was there in spirit as much as it was physically right next door. I found this out when hard times hit and I tried to change careers because my union job was being moved to Smithville, Tennessee, that my Associate's Degree wasn't enough. In 1986 my options were few, only to find myself working for a Jewish furniture store delivering furniture.

Drug dealing had overtaken Kinloch by the 80s and I had a wake-up call to stop smoking weed cold turkey. I just got tired of the monotonous routine of waking up smoking, all day smoking, and going to bed smoking. My wife had somehow taken my place as the family drug addict but took it to a new level. Crack was now the demon out to destroy our way of life and all that I could do was try to manage the fallout of constant deceptions and disappearing valuables.

Every night was a new battle for sanity as she left home like a vampire until the morning light. Before long I lost my home and had to move back to Kinloch. Once again, my parents put in a good word for me with the manager of the Kinloch Manor Apartments where I was able to move into the building right behind them. Here we tried to restore order to the family but my wife's sister got involved with one of the crack dealers and the nightmare returned only this time my niece and nephew, ages 9 and 12, were added to the list of casualties. My two daughters 12 and 14 were coping with my absence during the day at work and their mother's overnight. One evening my niece and nephew walked about 8 miles from where they lived to get to our apartment when neither my wife nor their mother were anywhere to be found. Together we managed to eat and survive the times of trouble that we found ourselves in the middle of. Soon we all were living in the same apartment together. Here we had my only son who was spared the fate of becoming a crack baby only by the grace of God.

At the same time that my wife was pregnant, her sister was carrying the baby of the crack dealer she had been living with. Soon after my son was born, I also had a new niece and we all wondered what was going on. I had been drug-free for over a year now and working my butt off at the furniture store delivering furniture and taking side jobs moving people with my boss's truck. Most moving jobs were moving rich friends of my boss or members of their family. Slowly I got to a weekly wage that I could provide some of the needs of our growing family but not without making loans from my parents from time to time.

I became determined to make my own way but the crack kept taking me backwards at every opportunity. The disease of drug addiction had been taking a toll on each member of the family so when my wife's mother who recently moved to Seattle, Washington, described a land of opportunity for her daughter, I began to form a plan to get my sister-in-law and her children where they could make a new start. I got one of those Capital One secured credit cards and was soon able to rent a van to drive us all to Seattle for my vacation. Only having one week for a vacation left me with one night to rest and start my journey home but I had to drive back solo while my family visited their grandma for two weeks then coming home later that month.

The trip home was almost without incident if it hadn't been for Ogden, Utah, where my gas stop resulted in a skinhead scare. When I gassed up someone must have noticed that I had out of state plates and most obvious that I was Black. No one else that I saw was Black for the entire time I was in Ogden but to my surprise I was being followed by a group of people in a couple of cars that drove around me in circles shouting racial names and throwing trash at my van. Before being followed I had been looking for something to eat like a McDonald's or something but my better judgment told me to wait until I find a truck stop further down the highway. Moments later the crowd around my van grew to several vehicles but I ignored them and looked desperately for the highway signs leading to the next town on my route home. This was long before GPS and cell phones so all I had was my map highlighted with highways and landmarks. It started to rain and I could see my highway signs just before it did but most of all my escort decided to seek someplace to put the top on the leader's convertible, ending the parade of vehicles that were so close to mine.

The only challenge beyond that point was staying awake and Pepsi became my constant companion until I reached home.

Saved & Sanctified

By now there was an active campaign to move residents out of Kinloch for airport expansion. Homeowners saw dollar signs and a push to disincorporate had begun. St. Louis County Housing Authority was leading the charge with Black women who knew the system painting a rosy picture of new construction in other parts of the county. Once again, the Belue Hadnot Apartments were front and center of a county vs. Kinloch issue. This time the competency of city officials and even corrupt elected officials were the focus of attention.

A federal law wouldn't allow the Belue Hadnot Apartments to be demolished unless another complex was built that matched the number of units already existing. The only way around the law was for the Kinloch board of Aldermen to vote in favor of an action called "Demolition Disposition" to abolish a number of public housing units.

After living in Kinloch a year and working with Mrs. Lucye T. Belue, my former high school principal, on the board of directors of a non-profit organization that operated the Kinloch High School building as a community center, I was eligible to run for office. My dad's seat on the board of alderman was available because they moved to Ferguson, so I ran for it and won. One of the issues that I ran on was the re-opening of Kinloch High School building as a community center, but only one month into my term someone burned down the historic building and no one has ever been convicted for the crime or any attempt made to rebuild the historic schoolhouse.

My election was in part an attempt to expose some of the obvious corruption in Kinloch's officials who must have been allowing the crack dealers to openly do business without local opposition from police or city officials. The only hope of Kinloch's survival was in saving its people from themselves and the drug epidemic that was profitable for some but devastating for everyone else. The drug market had gotten so bad that most of the day and all night people could drive through and the dealers or their addicts would run to random vehicles selling rocks like it was part of a toll road fundraiser.

When my wife and family returned from Seattle, she soon fell right back into her routine and pawnshop items started to disappear from our home. No one could have anything of value whether it was a gift or some prized possession that took months to save up for. We began to argue more and more until the idea of her going to Seattle to get clean began to make some sense. Our oldest girl was a senior in high school but she was willing to go with her mom and baby brother to help her kick the habit. My middle daughter was staying with me to continue her schooling but her older sister would have to finish her senior year in Seattle somehow.

My son and I were about as close as we could be and my heart broke into a thousand pieces when I saw them off at the train station. I gave them close to four months to get clean before my next vacation and in the meantime, I worked two jobs to get the money to drive up and bring them home. When my middle daughter and I made the drive to pick them up, we enjoyed most of the time on the road together until her gum popping got on my last nerve and I started making cow mooing sounds to get back at her. When we could get a radio station that played, we didn't complain about the kind of music that was on and in Rapid City we slept in the van for about five hours to rest on a hotel parking lot.

Seeing how much my boy had grown in such a short time was a shock but when we got there at 6:30 a.m., he was stretched out in the bed where he slept and I hugged him tighter than I think I ever did before. We saw some beautiful country on the way back including Mt. Rushmore and the Little Big Horn, but after being home only a few days it was obvious that crack still had my wife firmly in its grip.

It would take a total of eight years, two arrests, a divorce, and hitting the very rock bottom of her life to turn my now ex-wife's life around. She started rehab as part of a mandatory probation and it saved her life. Meanwhile, I kept my son as much as possible even as my older daughters struggled with their mom and both having babies of their own. The crack problem had taken a huge bite out of Black America, and Kinloch was right in the middle of it. My political involvement didn't even make a dent in Kinloch's drug trafficking but maybe there was hope for the historic value to return.

Soon after the mayor and other residing officials were indicted for various crimes, Bernard Turner was elected as mayor and a new board was faced with the task of voting on the "Demo Dispo" plan presented by a few Belue Hadnot residents and county lobbyist. St. Louis County and the Airport Authority of the City of St. Louis had plans to remove Kinloch from any official role in the redevelopment of the area surrounding Lambert International Airport. A map had been drawn that didn't include Kinloch as part of a master plan for redevelopment. Although I didn't see the map for myself, the events that took place during the late 80s and entire 90s showed evidence of an intent to remove both Kinloch and Robertson from existence.

Both of these communities were entirely Black populated and governed but they were told that the airport would be either buying them out or taking away their property by eminent domain due to airport expansion. Noise abatement was supposed to be the big reason that the areas needed to be vacated and the whole idea was being dressed up to look like an opportunity for prosperity and a better neighborhood for the families who moved early on in the whole campaign. This campaign was promoted just like a political machine was being called to action with lobbyist and scare tactics to influence the residents who owned their homes first then the low-income and subsidized housing tenants last.

Business owners, politicians, pastors, and any other community leaders were told about the hazards of waiting to accept relocation funds while the county and airport pressed on with their planned expansion. Various ideas had been tossed out to answer the question of why and how a runway expansion eastward into Kinloch could possibly make sense. One of the most ridiculous plans was to build a bridge runway over highway 170 even though the highway was fairly new itself and it seemed a natural border between the airport and Kinloch on the city's western outline of Hanley Road.

Now more than ever, Kinloch was being flooded with drugs and it's criminal elements that go along with it and many people were trying to escape the negative reputation that seemed to be growing with every news cycle. The same people who were part of Kinloch's most prosperous and strong brotherhood were starting to see greener grass outside of town. Family members were being called to testify against one another at Airport Authority hearings held in St. Louis City Committee Sessions. Rev. Larry Rice tried to sponsor homeless shelters in Kinloch and was opposed by lobbyist for the buyout who lived in Kinloch. These residents were homeowners who were also community leaders seeking quick buyout from the airport because they lived too close to subsidized housing and the property value was declining with each year they remained. I know this because I went out on patrol with one of Reverend Rice's volunteers and saw evidence that people had been sleeping in abandoned buildings at temperatures below zero when I was moved to testify against the buyout. Downtown at the city hall where I went for the hearing, my mother and two of her friends who also owned homes in Kinloch had come to testify in favor of the buyout and sat in the front row as I entered the room.

My plans to testify about the need for affordable and subsidized housing in Kinloch had been successfully derailed by my loyalty to the people who raised me. My mother and I quietly met in the hallway outside of the hearing where we told each other about our planned testimonies. She was prepared to say that life in Kinloch was becoming unbearable due to several hardships that the buyout could fix. She believed that my testimony would prolong the wait or stop the progress of her block being offered relocation funding. Kinloch was my home, but my mother was my family and I couldn't do anything to harm her idea of prosperity. So I told Rev. Rice that I couldn't oppose my parents at the hearing. He graciously understood and said my name would be removed from his witness list for that day.

Hanging my head in shame, I couldn't bear to stay and hear the results of my failed attempt to help Kinloch survive an obvious attack on 'its survival. My own family had fallen victim to the crack epidemic and I had a true prodigal son experience that brought me back to Kinloch when we had nowhere else to go. When the going got tough, Kinloch High School building was one place where tough people like Mrs. Lucye T. Belue could still be found but she had never even thought of being any place else and that's another story altogether. Mrs. Belue had been the principal of Kinloch High School since long before I was a student there. She had a sister named Sarah Smith who was feared to be unstable mentally but Mrs. Belue had enough sense for the both of them. She was loved by all who had ever attended Kinloch High.

I began my family as a resident in the Kinloch Housing Authority Projects known as the Belue Hadnot Apartments. Many other families found refuge from the rising cost of living in these buildings that were decent and affordable. When everyone else was trying to cut and run, the true blessing that those buildings stood for somehow got lost inside the prospect of financial gain and movin' on up with the Jeffersons.

I was just one of the "Boys Next Door to Ferguson" when Kinloch came under attack. This invasion was supposed to go quickly and smoothly but God obviously had other plans. The public housing units should have been the easiest to vacate and demolish. Many residents were scared away early in the process because the KHA (Kinloch Housing Authority) board had voted to accept a plan presented to them by the HASLC (Housing Authority of St. Louis County). This plan was called (Demo/Dispo) or Demolition/Disposition.

A Department of Urban Planning and Development Corporation was created to manage the entire moving campaign including the meet and greet, advisement, and payment of funds for relocation. As a newly elected Alderman, I was introduced to a Miss Julia Tibbs who held the office of Director of Grants and Operation Excel. Any time we had a meeting there was light refreshments like cookies, finger food, sandwiches, and soft drinks. People seemed to come to the meetings from the board of Alderman and residents of public housing to hear what the various options were available to them. Any suggestion to alter the nuts and bolts of the plan were deferred to a higher power that never showed its face. The housing authority office was the usual place of most meetings but these meetings were leading up to a very important meeting of the board of Alderman to vote upon acceptance of the Demo/Dispo plan that the housing authority board had already approved.

`When I attended these meetings, I began to ask questions pertaining to the need for public housing that would exist even after a buyout of current residents who accepted the offer to relocate. My common sense questions started to raise doubt among some of the people who attended the meetings. A defensive and at times hostile exchange began to take place between the Operation Excel, HASLC, Airport Authority, and myself.

One of the residents who seemed to be articulate, educated, and friendly with the lobbyist for the buyout was somehow convinced to run for a vacated alderman seat and she won at the end of the first year of my 2 year term. Ms. Geralda Smith and I became friends and talked about the buyout often. When the time came to vote on the Demolition/Disposition proposal, the lobbyists must have believed that they had the votes to approve it and not much else was being said or done about concerns that people who opposed the measure continued to raise.

Our small city only had four Aldermen and the Mayor who would vote to break a tie when one occurred. Ms. Smith, myself, Leonard Carter, and Kermit Robinson made up the entire board with Mayor Bernard Turner. On the date of the vote to accept the Demo/Dispo request, our auditorium was filled to its capacity with residents of the KHA apartments and homeowners who were waiting to be bought out. I was living in the Kinloch Manor Apartments with my family and Ms. Smith lived in the KHA Apartments with her children. Leonard Carter and Kermit Robinson lived in homes that would be bought by the airport, as did the Mayor who would break any tie if there would be one.

The meeting began with the reading of minutes from the previous meeting and we took care of some old business but finally the discussion of the Demo/Dispo plan was at hand and I gave my argument against allowing the demolition of decent and affordable housing just out of fear that the airport would expand deep into our city limits. The majority of people at the meeting seemed to be in favor of the plan and had adopted the catch phrase that to reject the plan would be, "...holding the residents hostage" against their will.

Mayor Turner wanted no part of a decision to deny residents an opportunity to leave if they wanted to move. Carter and Robinson spoke along the same lines but my response was always that the buildings were not being held hostage and were a separate issue. Ms. Smith never revealed a commitment to either viewpoint but was expected to follow the majority. Demolishing the structures would be irreversible but I believed that residents should be allowed to move without the condition of destroying property that could be used by other people. Before the vote was taken, there was time allowed for questions and comments from residents of the housing authority and citizens of Kinloch who were in attendance.

From the seated position we held above the crowd it was not hard to see that certain people were being given a signal to step up and speak and that the coaching was coming from Ms. Tibbs of Operation Excel in favor of the Demo/Dispo plan. The plan seemed like a done deal from all the discussion being so one sided, then Mr. Virgil Jones spoke and talked about his family who were blessed to have a home in the KHA. He went on to say that it would be a shame to allow the buildings to go to waste unless we were sure that there was no other alternative. Mr. Jones was a former resident of the KHA apartments who chose to buy his own home in Kinloch and didn't want to move.

Ms. Tibbs spoke and continued the fearful trend of describing a Kinloch that no one would want to live in and how the airport would take the property anyway if they didn't vote to demolish it. This had been a pretty effective argument for most of the campaign against saving the apartments but we were not going quietly. I had to ask what would be gained by tearing down decent affordable housing mainly because I didn't believe that the airport would be expanding into Kinloch and we were being" taken for a ride." Everything that Kinloch had of any value was gotten after a fight but now our big brother St. Louis County wanted to hand us a gift wrapped "Trojan Horse." I couldn't prove that there was an unseen motive behind the Demo/Dispo plan but nothing about its sudden push for approval was transparent.

Finally, it was time to vote and each alderman would be allowed to explain the reason for our vote. The mayor asked the city clerk to poll the board and the first to vote was Alderman Kermit Robinson. He began by telling us how difficult it is to decide what was best for Kinloch versus what was best for the residents of the housing authority. The airport had already made him an offer for his property and he told us that he felt uncomfortable voting so he would choose to abstain because he didn't want to appear biased.

Next came Alderman Carter a property owner who owned more than one lot being sold to the airport along with his own residence. He didn't have any concerns about his relationship with the Airport Authority as he repeated the reason for his vote to accept the Demo/Dispo. He said that he refused to hold the residents hostage and the crowd cheered in unison.

When my name was called everyone already knew how I was voting so I simply said that I vote no to the proposed plan. At this point the votes were tied and all eyes went to Ms. Smith as everybody could feel the tension when the clerk said her name. No one in the room expected she would need as much time to answer as she was taking but she was silent for almost a full minute before finally saying no loud enough to be heard by everyone. To my surprise and delight the looks on everyone's face said it all. Common sense had been given a chance over senseless greed. Hope was still alive.

At this point, the clerk announced that the motion had failed with a roll call of one abstention, one yes vote, and two no votes. The few people who had been vocal about not approving the plan were in shock but at the same time breathing a sigh of relief when the mayor announced his regrets that the vote turned out against Demo/Dispo.

He said that he would seek to find ways of helping residents who wanted to move but the board has expressed its pleasure in the matter.

So now the plan for demolishing enough of Kinloch to threaten its status as a fourth class city was stopped in its tracks and it was only due to the voices of a few people who gave a reasonable argument and believed that they could make a difference.

California Dreaming

The house where many years earlier I played with Ray and Adrienne was still occupied by the aunt who they lived with but she got sick and died. At the funeral, I saw both Ray and Adrienne. We were shocked and amazed at all that was going on in our lives, the most of which was that Adrienne was unmarried and had no children. She was still the California girl who I dreamed about and I pursued a long distance relationship with her that got very serious after my divorce.

Soon after my first trip to L.A., an opportunity to work for TWA was shown to me and I jumped at it for obvious reasons. Kinloch remained my home but now I was allowed to rent the house where Adrienne's aunt had lived for so many years.

Raising my son had become a priority for me but not without conditions. The most costly conditions came from having to share custody with his mother who hadn't kicked her crack habit yet. When I was at work, she had him and on my trips to L.A. he stayed with her.

I ended up being a one term alderman when I lost my next election but there was still hope for Kinloch's future as Mayor Turner began to see the county's plan for Kinloch through a different lens. He engaged the assistance of an older gentleman named William Gillespie who shared the view that Kinloch was still a very viable city with enormous potential. They could see that even after the failed attempt at Demo/Dispo the county was taking a different road to the same destination of Kinloch's eventual disincorporation.

To my surprise Mayor Turner appointed my neighbor Virgil Jones and me to serve on the Kinloch Housing Authority board of commissioners when two of the members who voted in favor of Demo/Dispo were relocated with Airport Authority funds. This created an opportunity to reverse the direction of public housing and start adding residents instead of losing them. Mr. Gillespie had experience in grant writing and was willing to help on several attempts to fund redevelopment of the slowly deteriorating buildings.

At this point the KHA consisted of three projects totaling the 225 units of housing, the Belue Hadnot (the oldest), the Dunbar Gardens (a senior citizen complex and the newest), then the Charles Folwell units (a mixture of family and senior dwellings). These buildings were being maintained as well as they could until they became vacant and the county housing authority knew that if money was offered to residents to move, they would take it.

One of the last votes taken by the Kinloch Housing Authority before Mr. Jones and I were appointed gave management rights to the HASLC and it included transfer of bank account authorization to the county. From there the newly appointed commissioners began to be treated like employees of the county without any authority to handle the business of property management. Here is where a struggle for survival began and St. Louis County was determined to eliminate any and all residents from the property and build replacement housing outside of the Kinloch city limits. Nothing that we did was given serious consideration if it included re-occupying the apartments located in one of the Housing Authority complexes. Our only alternative was to sue to regain our rights of authority.

Mayor Turner and Mr. Gillespie tried to assist the housing authority board in our attempt to get an attorney to help us but

HASLC would not release funding to pay for one. Our fight for survival was starting to show signs of progress until the mayoral election.

By this time HASLC began to change its strategy and started to look for a way to attack from the inside as it had done with Demo/Dispo. Here is where a name that was well known to most of Kinloch would play a major role in Kinloch's future. The Conways had been known to be successful businessmen because of their purchase of what had been called the "Threaded Needle" nightclub and bar. They renamed the entertainment business "The Cotton Club." Here was the spot to be every weekend and holidays for entertainment of every kind but even before the Cotton Club the Conway boys were known for their monopoly on the crack business in Kinloch. The nephew of these famous Conways was the featured DJ on many occasions and became popular with Kinloch customers but even before that I allowed him to hold dances at the Kinloch High Community Center when I was working with Mrs. Belue. If we had not been so deeply involved in our dispute against HASLC, I may have supported his run for mayor. But I didn't and when word got back to him that I was endorsing Turner, he was genuinely angry with me.

Just like any hearsay causes friendships to die we were now on a collision course and Keith Conway held on to his version of what he had heard about me even though we had been good friends before. When he won the election there was an immediate challenge to the authority that Mr. Jones and I had been building.

First Conway wanted to move into one of the senior citizen apartments and we opposed the idea because the units were built to accommodate handicapped and senior residents. Soon after our challenge to his new authority he requested to meet with Mr. Jones and me but the meeting was a disguise for his true intention.

Upon our arrival to his office, Conway seated us and asked what did we have to prove that we were even board members. As strange as that sounded Mr. Jones said that we had I.D. cards and Conway asked to see them which was even more odd. While Conway held Mr. Jones' card in his hand, he asked to see mine and I laid it on the table with my hand still on it when Conway forcibly snatched my card from my hand. As I stood to my feet and reached for a chair to hit him over the head with it a police officer hurried into the room and stopped me from my intended attack. Conway directed the officer to escort us out of his office as we exchanged insults and cursed each other.

Now we were in full battle mode and had several face to face encounters but none became as violent as the office visit that almost got very ugly. Mr. Jones and I were attempting to regain our board seats while challenging HASLC for authority to save public housing in Kinloch. The events leading up to this situation had to be orchestrated by political pros because they fed the ego of people in power and demonized anyone who even suggested opposition. The Conways began a new era of prosperity and political favoritism but HASLC had found a new friend who came at a bargain basement price. Our attempts to challenge Mayor Conway or HASLC fell flat mainly due to a lack of funding but that was certainly part of the plan.

My last ditch effort to save the Kinloch Public Housing came in the form of my own rehab of the vacant apartment right next door to one of the Aldermen on the board in Kinloch. I moved out of Adrienne's aunt's house and into the vacant unit made on the style of a duplex but I didn't have money to buy anything so using the pick-up truck that I had I began salvaging everything that I needed from other vacant units.

Soon my apartment was ready to have the utilities turned on and by God's grace everything worked perfectly. When I tried to offer a contract for rental to the new board of commissioners, they ignored me so I started sending them checks each month for $200 but my sole purpose for doing everything was to start opening up the apartments for others to move in. In the Charles Folwell Apartments, there were only one or two people still living in the units so when I moved in, Mayor Conway must have seen dollar signs and he took over management of the entire projects and made plans to re-occupy the rest.

For over a year I lived there with my son and sent checks that they returned until I got an eviction notice from the newly hired apartment manager. While living there I began publishing my own newsletter exposing the local leaders corrupt activities and even my campaign for challenging Conway in the next mayor's race. "The Watchdog" became popular and it must have aggravated Kinloch's politicians because they stepped up their attacks on me. When I attended board meetings, they would arrest me for asking questions and detain me until the meeting was over then let me go as a demonstration of the power they had.

My big brother died of an apparent heart attack, then the following year my hero passed away from the cancer that he had been battling for so long. When dad died, my mother was left with the house in Ferguson and I was the only boy to help care for it with her. So like most sons, I had already been cutting her grass, but now almost all of the maintenance was my job. I didn't mind, but my trips to L.A. slowed for a little while.

Adrienne and I had been going to Vegas to visit her dad who lived there regularly and taking trips everywhere. Sometimes we would take my son with us like when we went to Disney Land or San Diego Zoo, but I could tell he wasn't impressed he just wanted to be with his dad. On one of my birthdays, I left my son with his mother when Adrienne and I went to Catalina Island but when we got back to her place there were several messages on her answering machine for me to come home immediately.

Once I called my mom, she told me that all of my belongings were sitting on my front lawn at the apartment in

Kinloch. When I got home, nothing was there but my mother had paid someone to take my stuff to a storage facility until I got home. The strategy to divide and conquer was working for HASLC and Kinloch City Hall was playing their part. Now I was gone from Kinloch because I had to go to my mother's home and regroup.

The anger I felt was only surpassed by my determination to fight back. When I passed out my "Watchdog" newsletter I had gotten to be friends with the manager of the Boaz Apartment complex in Kinloch so when she saw that I was being harassed by the city officials, she offered me an apartment. This would be exactly what I needed to continue my newsletter and run for mayor so that's what I did and my campaign gained momentum when I started publishing every week instead of every month.

My job at TWA had gone through some hard times and we were bought out by American Airlines. This was becoming more of a blessing than a burden when we started getting more money and equipment in the following months. I still was able to travel to L.A. and take care of my boy and even help my daughters every now and then. Things were going almost too good until the attack on the Twin Towers hit and all air traffic came to a halt. On 9/11 I was enjoying one of my regular Tuesday off days but on 9/12, 13, and 14 all we did was clean aircraft and take breaks until flights were cleared again. We became the first trained TSA screeners and now we had to screen passengers before they could board our aircraft. The flights to L.A. had all but stopped cold while the entire industry was re-invented and our job description redefined. Somehow the word got out that I was publishing the "Watchdog" at work and people started calling me Watchdog even in Kinloch.

My campaign got pretty heated when I published a copy of a letter from Mayor Conway that accused him of overcharging his new tenants with that issue of the "Watchdog." He actually got nervous that I might be swaying voters away from his loyal group. Adding insult to injury, I applied for one of the apartments that I had been evicted from before. And when the mayor saw what I was doing, he displayed his anger by calling me insulting names as I filled out the application in the city hall. This was encouraging to me so I brushed off the insults while ignoring him and his assistant when they stood waiting for a reaction.

When April came, I lost the election but not by as much as expected. The following day a knock on my door led me to look through the peephole to see a policeman standing at my door. When I opened the door, the officer asked me to step outside so I did and he immediately put cuffs on my wrist then asked me to turn around for him to cuff the other wrist. I didn't resist because I was more curious as to the reason that a Kinloch police officer who routinely jokes with the local crack dealers was arresting me. When I asked him what I was being charged with he said "forgery" and to my utter surprise they were referring to my campaign literature with the mayor's signed letter included. The mayor was still mad about his letter being published with my "Watchdog" so he sent one of his officers to lock me up in Clayton.

Upon my arrival at the Clayton jail, I was placed in a holding cell with several other men who seemed content with the accommodations and knew the routine quite well. Being older than most of my companions I kept a serious face and stood ready to defend myself if it should become necessary. To my surprise there was no shortage of comedians standing ready to joke and poke fun at any and everything in sight. Names weren't mentioned unless more than one person was arrested together and that was very obvious because they would be talking strategy or just about things they all knew equally well. One of the young men caught me smiling and said that he knew he would get a laugh out of me and I was impressed. Impressed by the way so many Black people are still able and willing to make someone smile in the middle of what has to be one of the lowest points in his or her life.

Having been jailed before for a short period allowed me to remain confident that it wouldn't last long and patience was the most valuable tool that I possessed. For some reason, the male and female prisoners were allowed to share the common space in the middle of the area we were being kept in but I soon saw that it was a bad idea. As I reflect on what I witnessed the intention of the designers of the space must have been to tease the animal instincts of people locked away like savages. Here sat a young man in his early 20s and a woman nearly the same age talking as they sat in plain view of everybody when a younger male was brought in handcuffs and ankle cuffs got the attention of all of us because we had to go inside the cells until the guards finished releasing him from his cuffs. They put the young man in a cell with others and as the schedule went 15 minutes later the common area was reopened to us all.

The young Thunder Cat walked to a seat and sat near the young lady who was talking to the man in his 20s. They began to talk when the guy who was talking to her before walked up and said something to them both standing just in front of the two of them. I watched and could almost feel what was about to happen before it did. The Thunder Cat calmly stood to his feet and without warning began to pound the other guy with a series of lefts and rights to the temple and facial area before they were wrestling to the floor. It looked like the older guy was dazed but the Thunder Cat began to scream as the guards tried to separate them. He began to yell, "He's biting my nuts, man!!" and as blood ran down the face of the older guy it was clear that blood was also coming from the pants of the Thunder Cat even as the guards pulled them apart like opposing teams in a tug-o-war.

We were all put back into the overcrowded cells until the blood was cleaned up and the two fighters had been taken away for medical attention. When the common area was reopened, they offered us a bag lunch consisting of a thick slice of bologna on bread and some chips. Water was available from the fountain with a foam cup. I hadn't eaten all day so this was a welcomed meal for me. Without any evidence of forgery, I could not see how I would legally be kept here and after spending the customary 20 hours locked away, my name was called and I was released because no judge would sign the arrest warrant.

My niece had been able to find someone to cover my shift at work so when I got a ride home I picked up my son and returned to my apartment for the rest of the night. Instead of planning my revenge I decided to search the antenna channels for the new UHF network that had been advertised on billboards and commercials. UPN was a channel that I had watched in L.A. but was being expanded to the St. Louis area for the first time this week. While flipping through the channels I came across a network called 3 Angels Broadcasting Network that I had never seen before. The title of the program was being displayed behind the speaker as he talked about historical facts related to the Catholic Church and the commandment to keep the Sabbath Holy. For an entire hour without commercial interruption, I listened to Mark Finley discuss the topic of "Revelation Speaks Hope."

At the end of his study, I was crying like a baby because he had described my experience with the Catholic Church at Holy Angels School for the first part of my life. The things I had been taught and not taught about the historical accuracy of the Bible and the Commandments of God touched me to the bone and I kneeled beside my bed and prayed for God to reveal His will and His Word for my life. All of my anger and passion for revenge was gone and replaced with a passionate desire for a deeper understanding of God's instruction for life. It looked like my entire life had been wasted living without a true direction or knowledge of what is true and real. The most captivating message that I was hearing was that God would speak to me directly through His Divine Word and not to take the word of any man including the preacher. A fire was burning in my gut and the only thing that could control it would be the word of God.

When I spoke with Adrienne about my experiences, she was as respectful and understanding as could be. My next trip to L.A. was a little different because we went to see her father in Vegas, and while there her father and I found a Sabbath-keeping church to attend together. My conversations and entire thought process had become centered around learning more about God than I had previously believed. Our feelings for each other had not been shaken but I had clearly started down a path that I could not predict the future of.

Adrienne and I had plans to marry and live in St. Louis because the cost of living was cheaper and most of her family was living here. When I found a house in Northwoods, she gave me her own savings to help buy it and her brother Alden and I drove the U-Haul with her stuff in it all of the way to St. Louis non-stop. My daughters both had their own homes and I had a room at our house for my son so we were happy for a while until the word of God and my desire to share it with Adrienne became an issue. My desire was to live according to God's word but Adrienne believed that I was not ready for marriage so we slowly drifted further and further apart until she moved out.

By this time my mother had a stroke and was in a nursing home where she died and my older sister sold her house. With my share of the money, I gave Adrienne the money she had invested in our Northwoods home before she moved and we remained very close even after living apart. Now my focus was on reading the entire Bible and my relationship with God.

I joined the choir, became a deacon, and volunteered for every ministry the church could use me in. In the middle of all of my relationship issues I tried to return to work for American Airlines instead of the local company I had been working for but after only about six months of commuting between St. Louis and Chicago my health could not handle the pressures that the job demanded so I took early retirement. The financial burdens didn't allow me to remain in the house in Northwoods so I moved in with my daughter Sophia and my son lived with his mother while I sorted out my mess of a life.

As much as I loved Adrienne, her father shared his solemn belief that she would never marry me one weekend when I asked for his blessing upon our marriage. It took me a while to accept that truth but when I was faced with letting her go or continuing in sin the painful choice was the only one to make. My prayers are for her happiness and salvation but we each have to choose Jesus for ourselves.

EPILOGUE

A certain man went down... and fell among thieves which
stripped him of his raiment, and wounded him and departed
leaving him half dead." (Luke 10:30)
No names were changed to protect the innocent because
none of us are, least of all me. People should not be judged by
the tiny part they played in my life story either.
My mother was blessed to stand by her husband and family
faithfully until her death. John Davis has been a hero to
myself and others many times over and Glenda, my ex-wife
and ex-drug addict has become a most beloved model of how
to be a great grandmother and friend.
When Jesus returns will we still be trying to "Justify"
ourselves by asking, Him "Who is my neighbor?"
Ferguson's riots begged the question, " Do Black Lives Really
Matter?" Depending upon what race or social class is in
power the next question will be "Do Any Lives Matter?"

Tell Your Story and see if it matters!!

THE END